HOLIDAY IN EUROPE

A Studio Book

IN EUROPE

Photographs by Fritz Henle

Text by Anne Fremantle

with an Introduction by Patrick Dennis

THE VIKING PRESS · NEW YORK

*The photographs in this book are dedicated by
Fritz Henle to the memory of his mother.*

ACKNOWLEDGMENTS

Fritz Henle is indebted to many people for their
assistance in arranging schedules during his recent
tour and for providing other special facilities. Particular thanks are due to Birger Nordholm, Manolita
Dolger, Fred Birmann, Bruno Baroni, Franz Schwar-
zenstein, Jon Brower, José Cabral, and Oscar Bolin, and
also to Color Corporation of America, to Studio 13 in
Zurich, and to the Motal Custom Darkroom in New
York for their work in processing prints and film.

Published in 1964 by The Viking Press, Inc.
625 Madison Avenue, New York 22, N.Y.
Published simultaneously in Canada by The Macmillan Company of Canada Limited
Printed in Italy by Istituto Italiano d'Arti Grafiche, Bergamo
Library of Congress catalog card number: 62-17069

CONTENTS

INTRODUCTION

I F you long for faraway places, if you dream of drinks at dusk in some romantic Old World square, if you find it hard to pass a travel agency without a backward glance — then don't fail to read this book.

You could hardly ask for better touring companions than Anne Fremantle and Fritz Henle. Anne Fremantle is a gifted and graceful writer, author and editor of two dozen books and an indefatigable world traveler. Fritz Henle's dazzling photographs have been oh-ed and ah-ed over in *Life*, *Look*, *Holiday*, *Harper's Bazaar*, *House and Garden*, and almost any other prestige publication you might care to mention.

With these distinguished guides you will be escorted on two European tours — one to the South and one to the North.

On the first trip Anne Fremantle and Fritz Henle will show you Greece and its legendary islands. (But if you fancy Greece, may I advise you *not* to fancy it during torrid July and August.) They will take you through Italy from Positano to Rome, Siena, Assisi, Florence and Venice — even to what is literally and figuratively the little postage-stamp republic of San Marino (population, 15,000; area, 38 square miles). Then up to Austria — Vienna, Salzburg, Innsbruck — the southern part of Switzerland and the tiny principality of Liechtenstein (62 square miles), and down to the south of France to visit such fabled places as Avignon, Arles, Cannes, Nice and yet another never-never land, Monaco (59 square miles), famous for its roulette, its stamps, its visiting yachts, and for a Serene Highness fresh from Philadelphia.

Next through Spain — Cordova, Toledo, Madrid, Avila, Seville, Granada — down to that point on the Straits of Gibraltar where you can almost reach out and touch Africa. Then into Portugal, through Lisbon, Bejia, Coimbra, Belem, and finally — reluctantly, as they used to say in travelogues — facing home again on the shores of the Atlantic.

Now for the North.

After a breath of Ireland you will go to Scotland and Loch Ness (where Fritz Henle was not able to photograph the Monster, although your own luck may be better) and journey downward through England to the Druid monuments at Stonehenge, to the wonderful sights and dignified bustle of London, to a bit of Shakespeare at Stratford-upon-Avon, to the stately homes of England (Blenheim is here) and crumbling castles such as that of Edward I (nearly eight centuries old) at Caernarvon.

Now across the North Sea to visit the energetic Scandinavians on their amazing peninsula: Norway with its modern cities and its timeless fjords; Sweden with its lovely Stockholm — "The Venice of the North" to crib once again from those late, unlamented movie shorts — its medieval castles, its eighteenth-century palaces, its wave-of-the future apartment and office buildings.

Up to that peculiar territory known as Lapland, thence to Finland, famous for its valor, for its impossible language — but then all Scandinavian languages are impossible — and for a kind of steam bath called a *sauna* which is so excruciatingly painful that it must be good for you. Now for Denmark, which boasts excellent beer, delicious food, four and a half

million of the most literate people in the world, and six million bicycles. Here you will see the homes of Hamlet and Hans Christian Andersen, Odense, and beautiful Copenhagen.

Back on the mainland once again and Belgium, too picturesque to be true. But it *is* true. Then to Holland — or the Netherlands if you prefer — to visit Gouda (cheese), Amsterdam (canals), Haarlem (chocolate), Scheveningen (fish), Delft (china), Rotterdam (Erasmus) and Alkmaar (see Gouda). And now for Germany, or as much of it as is currently on display — Cologne, Heidelberg, Munich, Oberammergau, to mention only a few of the stopping points. Finally you will swing into France, through its wine regions, its fairy-tale château country and, last of all, to every tourist's idea of heaven — Paris.

If you have been to all of these places, if you have a hankering to go, or if you never leave your easy chair, *Holiday in Europe* is the book for you. Big and beautiful, with 160 photographs — 74 of them in colour — and a lively text that will give you more interesting information than you are likely to get from the average guide book, *Holiday in Europe* is a pure delight for globe-trotter and stay-at-home alike. I recommend it highly.

PATRICK DENNIS

8

SOUTHERN EUROPE

GREECE

WHENEVER possible, one should begin at the beginning. This is true of history, of biography, of travel. The best way to start a holiday in Europe, therefore, is to land in Athens, which represents the very beginning of European civilization. For, though Europe is a land mass, the second-smallest continent, it is above all a spirit, a spirit epitomized by three female figures — first, Pallas Athene, the foundress and protectress of Athens, goddess of wisdom, who, legend has it, sprang perfect, complete and armed, from the forehead of her father Zeus, greatest of all the Greek gods; second, the Virgin Mary, "our fallen nature's solitary boast," as Wordsworth wrote, venerated by the Greeks, who call her *Theotokos*, mother of God, *Panagia*, most holy, and *Platitera tou Ouranou*, greatest in the whole universe; and third, the spirit of Liberty, symbolized in familiar feminine form and invoked by freedom-loving peoples throughout the world. These three figures represent the true "inwardness" of Europe. All are very much present in Greece,

the cradle of democracy and home of philosophy and technics, the very names of which are Greek.

There is no better place to land in Greece than at Athens airport, for your plane flies in over Homer's wine-dark sea, the Aegean, studded with bare, cobalt-blue islands. Circling to land you see the Parthenon, house of the Virgin Athena, sitting whitely on the Acropolis, high above the modern city.

The major theme of Greece is light. After landing, one steps out into the dazzling white, into a vast dreamlike brightness which pervades the entire southern part of the Balkan Peninsula. Greece is a small country, the area, including the islands, totaling about 51,200 square miles. There are today about eight million Greeks, and almost all win their livelihood directly from the land or the sea. Geography has been good to them. High, bare hills with few passes prevented invasions from the north; many inlets and sheltering islands made seafaring a pleasure and always profitable, from the time of Ulysses

9

up to that of today's Onassis. And from pre-Homeric Athens to the Piraeus of *Never on Sunday*, sailors have been heroes here — and have been at home.

The Acropolis is the most famous site in Europe. On it are the Parthenon, built between 447 and 438 B.C., in Doric style; the Erechtheum, built between 421 and 405 B.C. in Ionian style and today possessing five of its original caryatids, named after the town of Caryae from which the girl models came; the Propylaea, an ante-temple, begun by Pericles in 437 B.C.; and the small temple of Athena Nike, destroyed by the Turks in 1687 and recently reconstructed. Lord Elgin purchased this temple's frieze, like that of the Parthenon, and removed it early in the last century. The Parthenon's roof was blown off in 1687 after the occupying Turks used the building as a powder magazine, and many columns were hit by cannonballs in the war of 1827. Yet it still remains, as the Victorian John Addington Symonds described it, "the finest edifice on the finest site in the world, hallowed by the noblest recollections that can stimulate the human heart." On the hill of the Acropolis men attained, collectively, the highest they have ever attained, in thought, in art, in behavior, and in expression. To the south stands the Theater of Dionysus, where the plays of Aeschylus, Sophocles, Euripides, and Aristophanes were first performed, and to the north, the admirably restored Agora (market).

The Temple of Theseus, near the Thesion Station, is the most perfectly preserved temple in Greece. Though shaken out of line by earthquakes, none of the columns has fallen, and nothing more perfectly represents the glory that was Greece than the views to be seen here of the Acropolis, crowned by the Parthenon, of the slopes of Mount Hymettus, Mount Pentelicus, Mount Lycabettus, and of the nearer Areopagus. This last hill, consecrated to Mars and the Eumenides, or Furies, was the seat of the supreme court. It was here that Demosthenes was condemned in 324 B.C.; here that St. Paul told the Athenians that the Unknown God they worshipped was Him "in Whom we live and move and have our being." It was also to this hill that Orestes came after killing his adulteress and murderess mother, Clytemnestra.

Orestes' home was Mycenae, craggily set high between two impregnable hills in Peloponnesus, about seventy miles from Athens. Discovered by Schliemann, the palace of the Atridae is now dated around 1250 B.C. Recently a road was discovered leading to Agamemnon's palace, whose Lion Gate still shows the grooves from the door's hinges, and the stones below it the wheelmarks of the chariots that rolled in. Mycenae is the most breathtaking palace imaginable, worthy of the family that once inhabited it, and of the literature that has paid tribute to it since. The treasure, mostly of beaten gold, is now in the Athens museum; the masks, if not of Agamemnon and his cousin Aegisthus, date from their era.

Near Mycenae are new Corinth, with its fantastic canal, and the high, windy, ancient city (far from its snug modern namesake) where St. Paul also preached. This is a country of rich vineyards, of fields where shepherdesses still spin, and of wonderful beaches along the coast, such as Xylocastron and Kallini. To the south, on its own bay, is Nauplia, where the first independent Greek government functioned. Above it stands a Venetian fortress, and in its harbor another fortress on the island of Bourdzi, home of the executioner and now a delightful hotel and restaurant. From Nauplia it is an easy journey to Epidauros, the most perfectly preserved of Greek theaters; a whisper from its stage can be heard on the highest steps. Here also is the temple of Aesculapius with its strange *tholos*, a marble rotunda with Doric columns dedicated to the doctor who became a god after his death.

Crossing Peloponnesus to Olympia, one can go either through Arcadia, or, farther south, through Sparta. Set in a green valley through which two rivers flow, Olympia was a sanctuary of Zeus from before 776 B.C. until the fifth century. Ruins of the twelve treasure houses built by the Greek states can be seen here, as well as the temple of Hera, the site of Phidias's studio, and the theater where the Olympic games took place every four years. The peaceful Olympia museum contains the famous Hermes of Praxiteles and Apollo and the Centaurs.

Also in Peloponnesus is the medieval town of Mistra, crowded with churches, many of which contain admirable Byzantine mosaics. The ferry from Patras to Itea provides one approach to Delphi, "the center of a colossal enclosure of bare rocks, naturally shaped like a theater; the temple splendidly dominates the tragic solitude," as Strabo noted. To some, Delphi represents the single most perfect expression of Greek culture. Old even in Neolithic times, Delphi was consecrated to Apollo, the sun god, whose Pythian priestess sat prophesying high on a sacred tripod while vapors arose from fissures in the chalk below her. After washing his feet in the cold water of the sacred Castilia spring, today's voyager can see the remains of the ancient temple of Apollo, its terraces linked by a sacred way. High above are the stadium and the theater, and far below the *tholos* and two Doric temples of Athena. Outside the modern museum is the earliest Christian mosaic in Greece, and inside the great bronze charioteer.

Thebes, city of Oedipus and of Antigone, is on the road back from Delphi to Athens; the stone lion of Chaeronea still stands at the crossroads. Nearby, Ossios Loucas, a Byzantine monastery with good frescoes, can be visited in summer; nearer Athens is Daphni, another monastery with eleventh-century frescoes, and Eleusis, site of the Mysteries, where ruins of the temples of Demeter and Persephone still stand. Eleusis looks out over the bay of Salamis, scene of the tremendous battle of 480 B.C. when about three thousand Persian ships, commanded by Xerxes, who had occupied Athens, were defeated by one-tenth the number of Greek ships under Themistocles. On the other side of Athens, past the lovely beach of Glyfada, is Sounion, where the sea god Poseidon's shining marble temple dominates the view from a cape holy even in Homeric times.

The cave monasteries of Greece are famous. Those of Meteora can be visited by both men and women, those of Mount Athos by men only; the rules even state that hens are forbidden, let alone cows! The island of Rhodes with its Crusader castle and Valley of Butterflies is less than two hours by air from Athens, as is Crete with yet more treasures. For those with time, all the islands of the eastern Mediterranean can be seen on an Odyssey tour. These cruises set out from Piraeus, the port of Athens, just as the Greek ships sailed from it in the days of old.

ITALY

BOOT-SHAPED Italy has 116,228 square miles of land, and more than forty-seven million warm-hearted people. To the north, the Alps separate her from France, Switzerland and Austria; down her middle are the Apennines. While Greece is Europe's soul and its source, Italy is its unifier, for Rome gave most of Europe its laws, its roads, and its language. South of Rome, all of Italy was once *Magna Graecia* — greater Greece; the earliest temple at Paestum was built by the Greeks in the sixth century B.C. Sicily, too, is full of Greek ruins: Syracuse, Agrigento, Taormina, and perhaps best of all, Segesta, with its perfect temple high on a dry bare hill. But Greece is not the only influence in Sicily. In its capital, Palermo, are the most complete series of mosaics anywhere, crowned with the great glittering Christ Pantocrator of Monreale, monuments to the color sense of the Norman kings. The Cappella Palatina is a jewel of Arab-Norman architecture and the cathedral in Palermo enshrines the red porphyry tomb of the Emperor Frederick II, the *stupor mundi*, who was born in the lovely country of Apulia, south of Bari.

The "new city" of Naples, founded in the eighth century B.C., is the third largest town in Italy. A city of startling contrasts, it has unbelievable slums, glorious views, splendid museums, and Vesuvius too close for comfort. Pompeii and Herculaneum, preserved by the lava that killed their inhabitants in the year A. D. 79, look exactly as they did the summer they were destroyed. Boat excursions from Naples will take you to the lovely island of Capri, with its famed Blue Grotto, or to Ischia with its mud baths. On the mainland it is a short drive from Naples to Sorrento and to Positano, steep and white, its round-roofed houses set in citrus orchards with waves of fragrant blossoms foaming into the very sea. The Amalfi drive, one of the most beautiful in the world, leads to Amalfi itself, with its own Green Grotto and a cathedral with a shining majolica steeple visible for miles around.

And so at last, since all roads lead to her, *urbs et domina* — city and queen — "*Ecco Roma*," as the postilions used to cry, pointing their whips at the first sight of her. Today's Rome is a city of bells and buses and bicycles, of noisy Vespas with boy in front and girl behind, recalling the Sabine women whom the early Romans carried off; of immense flowering oleanders lining the modern streets; of dark ilexes and splashing fountains, of chattering swifts which darken the sky at sunset. Even on the dustbins are the magic initials of the City: SPQR — *Senatus Populusque Romanus*, the Senate and People of Rome, initials which today's smiling Italians like to reinterpret as: *Sono Porchi Questi Romani* — what pigs these Romans are!

Much of Rome can be seen by driving up and down the seven hills. The Colosseum, completed in 80 A.D., is a monument to much of the vilest cruelty ever systematically perpetrated; the nearby arch of Constantine was built after the Emperor's victory at the Milvian Bridge which converted him to Christianity. And then, of course, there is the Forum. This was once a small, level swampy place, chosen by Romulus as a meeting and market place for Romans and Sabines, when their war was done. The Forum is grassgrown now; most of the colored marbles were pilfered for use in other buildings. Three columns remain from the temple of Castor and Pollux, and more is left standing of the temple of Antoninus and Faustina. There are charming baroque churches nearby; also the arch of Titus and the large Victor Emmanuel wedding cake of a monument.

Rome's attractions are for all ages and tastes — the basilicas of St. John Lateran, St. Mary Major and St. Paul; the Piazza del Popolo; the Campidoglio designed by Michelangelo around the great statue of Marcus Aurelius; the Quirinal; the Scala Santa; the Pantheon; the Circus Maximus; the baths of Caracalla, and nearby the Food and Agriculture Organization (FAO), with its excellent roof-restaurant; Trajan's column and his market, where those who care for them feed the cats; the Fountain of Trevi, where everyone's penny should be ready if he wants to come back again; the Capitol, once saved by geese; the Spanish Steps; the eight remaining arches of Rome and the city walls; the Baths of Diocletian and the splendidly designed modern railroad station. Then, of course, there are the Villas Borghese and Medici; the Ara Pacis; the Piazza Navona, which used to be flooded for water carnivals; Hadrian's Bridge of Sant' Angelo and the Castle beyond; and the great Piazza of St. Peter's, with its glory of pillars and perfect symmetry. So much can be seen from the outside. But beware when you go inside, for three days can become three years before you escape! However, the insides of the Catacombs, the Sistine Chapel, and St. Peter's are a minimum requirement. If you can, add to your list in Rome the

Appian Way, the most history-crowded road on earth, and a trip to Hadrian's Villa and to the Villa d'Este with its unbelievable display of tiered gushing fountains in nearby Tivoli.

From Rome, excellent trains and buses will take you to medieval Siena or Assisi, both wonderfully set on high hills. Siena's thirteenth-century cathedral, in Alcatraz-striped marble, has a façade by Giovanni Pisano, sculptures by Bernini, and Donatello's exquisite St. John, with Pinturicchio frescoes in the library and a fantastic pavement of polychromic marble engravings. Siena has, too, a pleasantly unsymmetrical square, the Campo, where once in July and once in August the Palio is held, a race in which the riders gallop their horses through the town and the townsfolk wear medieval costumes and fling their caps in the air in wild excitement. In the Pinacoteca museum are six hundred Sienese paintings. The town is crowded with old buildings and steep, narrow, winding streets up which motorists think nothing of speeding. St. Catherine's little house and her shrine are here too.

Assisi is the most single-minded of all cities. Down near the station is the Portiuncula chapel which St. Francis repaired with his own hands; a church has been built over it and over the cell in which he died. Dominating the town is the great double church with its superb frescoes by Giotto, Cimabue and Simone Martini. In the Portiuncula St. Francis received the nineteen-year-old girl who became St. Clare and whose body still lies in the crypt of the church of Santa Chiara. Three miles uphill is the Carceri, the hermitage where St. Francis retired to pray in solitude. Here in spring the blue scillas come up through the snow.

Across the valley and overlooking the Tiber is Perugia, with its collection of Umbrian paintings, its great fountain with reliefs by Nicola and Giovanni Pisano, and the tomb of the Volumni, the finest extant Etruscan sculpture. At Arezzo, where Petrarch and Vasari were born, twice a year, in June and September, the Joust of the Saracens takes place,

a traditional medieval tournament rivaling Siena's Palio in pageantry and excitement.

Florence, glorified by the Medicis, claims to be the most beautiful city in the world. Certainly it has attracted, and produced, more great men than any city not a nation's capital. For a breathtaking view, go up to San Miniato, or to the Piazzale Michelangelo just below, or, best of all, to the Fortezze Belvedere above the Boboli Gardens, and look down on the most glorious set of tiled roofs imaginable, in all shades of buff and beige and russet, from the great dome of the Cathedral and Giotto's campanile to the shop-lined Ponte Vecchio, where sooner or later everyone goes to buy jewelry and trinkets.

In the center of Florence is the Palazzo Vecchio, where Cosimo de' Medici had offices as Podesta in the fifteenth century. Outside it a copy of Michelangelo's David and Cellini's Perseus can be viewed agreeably over lunch at one of the square's attractive outdoor cafés. Just off the square, past stands of tempting leather goods — a speciality of Florence — is the Uffizi Gallery, which houses one of the richest art collections in the world. Among hundreds of masterpieces hang Botticelli's *Birth of Venus* and his *Primavera*. The Pitti Palace, too, displays pictures and furniture. In the Medici chapels you will find Michelangelo statues; in the Palazzo Riccardi, paintings by Benozzo Gozzoli; in San Marco frescoes by Fra Angelico; in Santa Croce, the tombs of Michelangelo and Galileo. In Settignano is I Tatti, the house that art historian Bernard Berenson left to Harvard. It is one of the many beautiful villas that line the hills of Florence, almost all of which can be visited for a small fee.

No less an attraction to tourists than Florence is Venice. Divided in two by the Grand Canal and traversed by more than a hundred and fifty canals of various sizes, built right into the waters of the Adriatic, Venice is one of the great wonders of the world. St. Mark's Cathedral, erected in the eleventh century on the site of the small wooden church that was built in about 830 to house the saint's body, is Byzantine, decorated with mosaics, Gothic tabernacles, sculptures, and five glittering Oriental domes. It stands in the city's only piazza, an immense outdoor drawing room, enclosed on three sides by arcades and perpetually crowded with people and pigeons. The Ducal Palace's shimmering Gothic exterior of pink and white marble is lightened by large windows and balconies, and is joined by the Bridge of Sighs to the infamous jail from which Casanova escaped. A few gondola-lengths away from the Palace is the Royal Danieli Hotel, world-famous for bed, board, and some of the best spaghetti ever. The Accademia di Belle Arti contains many Bellinis and the most important collection of Venetian paintings in the world. Many of the best single pictures, however, are to be found in the churches. Santa Maria della Salute, Longhena's seventeenth-century church, has Titians and a Tintoretto, while San Sebastiano has its wonderful Veroneses.

Gondolas provide the most romantic transport, and the *vaporetti*, steamer buses, motor boats, and ferries the swiftest. The light in Venice — *nacrée*, or mother-of-pearl — is always different from that of any other place, and at sunset the palaces and houses that line the canals turn unbelievable colors.

The Lido is all — or nearly all — it is claimed to be, and elsewhere around Venice are lovely, little-known beaches, of which the Lido di Jesolo is a good example. Within easy reach of Venice are colorful towns such as Ravenna and Rimini, and San Marino, the oldest republic in the world, perched on dizzy heights overlooking the Adriatic. Directly en route to Milan is Saint Anthony's Padua, and Verona with its Romanesque church of San Zeno — Bernard Shaw's favorite — a complete arena (where bicycle races are held), and the tomb of Romeo and Juliet.

Many visits to Italy start and many end with Milan, the second-largest and most modern city, with its brand-new airport close to town. The biggest sight is a confectioner's dream of a cathedral, and the most treasured is Leonardo da Vinci's well restored *Last Supper* in the monastery of Santa Maria delle Grazie. Everywhere fabulous shops reflect northern Italy's great prosperity and abundant good taste in furniture, clothes and every kind of accessory. December is the month for music lovers to be here for the opening of the opera season at La Scala.

Everywhere in Italy good fun and glory are crowded into little space, but even half a day spent in one or another place can provide lifetime impressions: Rome, Florence, Venice, Pisa, Lake Como, Rapallo, Portofino, Orvieto, Bologna — no matter where you go in Italy, you will be happy you were there.

AUSTRIA

FROM Venice to Vienna is a day's drive through the high-peaked Dolomites. Austria is the heart of Europe, and Vienna, for centuries the capital of the Empire that Gibbon so rudely said was "neither Holy, nor Roman, nor Empire," is thoroughly cosmopolitan, gay and prosperous today. The city at the center of ancient trade routes was, and still is, the traditional meeting place of the East and West.

Today Vienna is as close as most Westerners come to the Iron Curtain — Russian-controlled territory lies within sight of it. There are many marvelous shops, and tempting coffeehouses and restaurants where coffee topped with whipped cream, Schlagober, new *Heurige* wine and the local specialities such as *goulash*, *schnitzel* and *strudel* should be sampled. Viennese cooking is superb, the pastries irresistible.

Vienna is emotion to Paris's intellect — softer, sweeter and baroque. The city's greatest expression lies in neither art nor literature but in music, which is not, as someone remarked, all "waltz and shmaltz," for here by the Danube lived Haydn, Mozart, Beethoven, Gluck, Bruckner, Brahms and Schubert, as well as the Strausses. Beethoven wrote the *Eroica* in Vienna. *Fidelio* was first given in Vienna in 1805, *Fledermaus* in 1874, and Viennese operagoers have heard most if not all of the great singers of our times.

The inner city is circled by the Ringstrasse, a magnificent tree-lined boulevard. St. Stephen's Cathedral, badly damaged in World War II, has been restored and its 450 foot high Gothic tower, the Stephen's Turm, begun in 1147, remains one of Vienna's great landmarks. Hapsburg treasures to be seen in the Hofburg include Charlemagne's crown, his sword and Gospels, and a sword of Harun-al-Rashid. The Library contains an impressive collection of eighty-one thousand papyri, thirty-four thousand manuscripts, and over a million books. In the Hofburg too is housed the Atomic Energy Commission. The Albertina Museum, with one of the best collections of drawings in the world, the House of Parliament, the university, and the Belvedere, Pallavicini and Liechtenstein palaces should be visited too. Of special interest to horse lovers is the Spanish Riding School, founded in the sixteenth century by Prince Eugene of Savoy. The unique Lippizaner horses perform daily except in August. There are lovely excursions around Vienna, to Heiligenstadt, Melk and St. Florian, above all to Schönbrunn, the summer palace of the Emperors.

One of the most-visited places in Austria is Salzburg, with its castle set like a diadem on a mountain. The city is delightfully baroque and built in tidy squares that lead one into another. You can ride through them all in a fiacre. Salzburg's italianate Cathedral is the perfect setting for the Mozart Masses performed in no other church. Outside, in the great square the medieval *Everyman* is expertly performed on sunlit afternoons during the festival, and in the evening Mozart's operas are sung. The composer's house stands near the Mozarteum, the famous summer school of music. Also, make sure to visit the lovely Mirabel Gardens. Nearby are Hellbrunn, a 1613 palace with an open-air theater in the formal seventeenth-century gardens, and Leopoldskron, another lovely palace offering open-air concerts.

In Innsbruck, the capital of the Austrian Tyrol and its ski center, mountains can be seen at the end of every street. It is a city of fountains and of picturesque delights, one of which is the Goldenes Daecherl (little roof), a small Gothic balcony three stories high with a steeply pitched glittering roof of gold under which the Emperor Maximilian introduced his newly chosen wife to his people. Arcaded streets and lovely ironwork are typical of Innsbruck. In the Hofkirche, bronze figures guard the Emperor Maximilian's tomb, which is surrounded by twentyfour marble reliefs representing events in his life.

From Innsbruck trains and buses go to all the ski resorts, Igl, Obergurgl (where you can ski as late as May), the Arlberg, the Zillertal, Ötztal and Vorarlberg. To the north of Austria is the Bohemian forest, running along the hills of the Czech border and broken by lovely medieval towns such as Gmunden. And to the south, Carinthia, one of the sunniest parts of Europe, can be reached over the splendid Gross Glöckner road. On Sundays and feast days, and at folk gatherings in the Tyrolean villages and towns, lovely embroidered costumes are worn by the natives in styles that have remained in fashion for hundreds of years. Nearly everywhere you stay in Austria you are sure of a warm welcome, for Austrians are charming, courteous and kind. If you go from Austria to Switzerland by way of the road that winds from Feldkirch in the Vorarlberg to Ragaz in the Canton of St. Gallen you will pass through the German-speaking land of the princes of Liechtenstein. Created as a separate principality within the Holy Roman Empire in 1719, Liechtenstein became a sovereign state in 1806, joined the German confederation in 1815, and has been independent since 1866. Its history, cloaked in many disguises, lurks in the plot of many a romantic novel and operetta.

Liechtenstein was allied with Austria before World War I, and its affairs were administered from Vienna and Innsbruck; today its currency, customs, and postal and telegraph services are all Swiss.

SWITZERLAND

SWITZERLAND is the still center at the core of Europe's turmoil, the quiet at the heart of its political and emotional hurricanes, the small, hospitable country that has always been a place of refreshment and peace. From the beginning, men have found refuge here — from themselves, like Rainer Maria Rilke, or from the tyranny of their fellow men, like Voltaire, Rousseau, Lenin and Klee. Europe trusts the Swiss, and the traveler trusts them too. It is one country where no car need be locked, where no one need check his valuables, and where you can drink with safety from every stream, tap and fountain.

Without the Alps there would be no Switzerland, and most of the country's 15,940 square miles containing twenty-two federated cantons are far from flat. Switzerland was founded in 1291, and is the second oldest republic in the world. It gave the world the Red Cross, and the first chance of peaceful coexistence through the League of Nations, housed at Geneva.

The standard of living is high, of literacy one hundred per cent. French, German, Italian, Romansh and English are spoken in many places, especially in the hotels, which are run with clockwork efficiency. It is the country of sport; skiing, mountain-climbing, water-skiing, swimming, sailing, motor-boat racing, fishing, golf, tennis, riding, shooting and dancing are as enthusiastically indulged in by the natives as by the tourists who flock there year after year.

The Swiss towns are delightful and each has its own special flavor. Schaffhausen on the right bank of the Rhine is German, and so is Altdorf with its monument to the Swiss hero William Tell. St. Gallen near Appenzell, with its Benedictine Abbey, was developed in the eighth century around a cell built in the seventh by St. Gall, an Irish monk who brought Greek back to Europe and taught it to the mainland clergy. The Abbey Church, rebuilt in 1765, is a miracle of baroque architecture and the library one of the oldest and most famous in Europe. Einsiedeln is a medieval pilgrimage place. Zurich, the largest Swiss city, is an international banking and insurance center with an old and a modern section, good schools, theaters, sport, museums and hospitals, and the best air service on the Continent. Most round-the-world flights stop here. Many high Alps are visible from the city, and during a flight over them to Italy, Tiefenkastel, near the Julier and Albula passes, can be seen. Zwingli, who with Calvin introduced the Reformation, was a native of Zurich, and there is a museum named after him.

Basel, on the Rhine, is Switzerland's second-largest town and is noted for its chemical industry. It is the home port of the Swiss merchant fleet. Erasmus, Calvin and Nietzsche lived there, as well as the artist Holbein, many of whose superb portraits are kept with other old and modern master works in the Art Museum. The eleventh-century cathedral is surrounded by delightful old buildings. Bern, Switzerland's capital in the shadow of the Bernese Alps, is well preserved from medieval days. It abounds in handsome towers, including the famous Clock Tower.

(Continued on page 81)

ATHENS:
The Parthenon.

18

MYCENAE: The Lion Gate of Agamemnon's Palace.

CORINTH: Remains of temples in the Old City, where St. Paul later preached.

PELOPONNESUS: Shepherdess spinning.

Right: NAUPLIA: Venetian fortress of Bourdzi.

ATHENS: The Water Carrier,
statue from the Agora.

EPIDAURUS: The most perfectly preserved of Greek theaters.

ATHENS: The Agora with reconstructed marketplace; behind, Mount Lycabettus.

PIRAEUS: Fishing nets drying.

ITALY

Left: ROME: Temple columns in the Forum. *Below:* Fountain of Trevi.

Overleaf: ROME: Colosseum; sunset over St. Peter's.
On the following pages: The temple columns at PAESTUM; the Temple of Apollo at POMPEII, with Vesuvius behind.

SIENA: The old Palace; pageantry of the Palio.

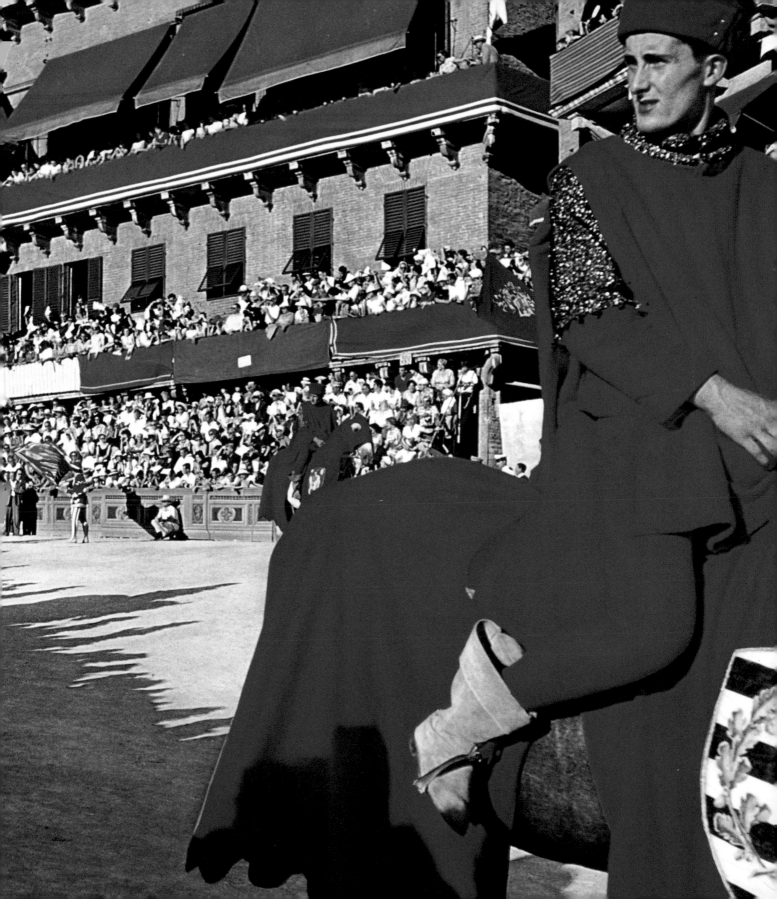

ASSISI: Steps up to the church of St. Francis.

SAN MARINO: Guard at the Palace.

Overleaf: FLORENCE: The Duomo, with Giotto's campanile at left.

VENICE: Spaghetti and red wine on the Royal Danieli Hotel terrace.

Opposite: Gondolier on the Grand Canal.

Campanile and horses of St. Mark's.

Gondola prows.

VENICE:
Santa Maria della Salute.

42

AUSTRIA

VIENNA: Schönbrunn from the park.

VIENNA: Inside the Belvedere Palace.

VIENNA: Main entrance of the Belvedere Palace.

VIENNA: View from St. Stephen's Cathedral.

INNSBRUCK: View from the Stadthaus Tower.

SALZBURG: View from the Mirabel Gardens.

INNSBRUCK: View of the Goldenes Daecherl.

VIENNA: Roof of St. Stephen's Cathedral.

INNSBRUCK: Bronze figures guard Emperor Maximilian's tomb.

SWITZERLAND

APPENZELL: View from Eben Alp.

LUGANO: The lake and city.

VALAIS: Picnic at Evolène.

TIEFENKASTEL: Near the Julier and Albula passes.

ALTDORF: Monument to William Tell.

BERNESE OBERLAND:
View from the Diavolezza.

LAKE OF GENEVA: Chillon Castle.

LIECHTENSTEIN: The Castle and the Rhine Valley.

LAKE OF LUCERNE: Looking
toward the Saint Gotthard Pass.

EINSIEDELN: Open-air play at the Monastery.

TARASP: Women in Engadine costume.

ST. MORITZ: Spires, flowers, and clouds.

AVIGNON: Fresh French bread.

LA TURBIE: Roman remains.

MONACO: Guarding Prince Rainier's Palace.

Right: CANNES: Yacht harbor and Casino.

EZE: Above Nice.

ARLES: The Roman theater.

SPAIN

CORDOVA: Roman bridge across the Guadalquivir.

TOLEDO: El Greco's view.

MADRID: In the Prado, copying Goya's *Maja*.

AVILA: The city gates.

SEVILLE: Bullfighter's cloak.

MADRID: Statue of Don Quixote
and Sancho Panza.

SEVILLE: The Giralda tower.

GRANADA: Alhambra reflections. *Right:* Flamenco dancer.

Overleaf: STRAITS OF GIBRALTAR: Facing Africa.

PORTUGAL

LISBON: Fronteira Palace and gardens.

Left: LISBON: Casa de los Bucos.

LISBON: The Old City.

BEJA: Windmill.

SESIMBRA: Fishermen bring in the catch.

LISBON: Fado singer in the Fronteira Gardens.

LISBON: Belem Tower on the River Tagus.

PRAIA DA ROCHA:
Atlantic beach.

(Photos: Tom Hollyman)

PLAIN OF TIPPERARY: Rock of Cashel.

IRELAND

COUNTY KERRY.

The main thoroughfare is lined with lovely arcades which face the colorful pillared fountains. Bern also boasts a wonderful zoo where the animals are kept as free as possible and the bears, particularly, have delighted spectators since the Middle Ages. Interlaken, between the lakes of Thun and Brienz, is the gateway to the Bernese Oberland, where rise the Eiger, Mönch, Jungfrau and Wetterhorn — giant mountains to climb or merely to stare at in wonder. The lakes, such as the lake of Lucerne, are as lovely as the mountains.

The valleys in Switzerland are marvelous too. In the Simmenthal in April the fields of fresh white narcissus and woods filled with lovely Swiss lilies of the valley and cyclamen, and, higher up, carpets of blue gentian, prove that the Swiss picture postcards and calendars of flowers, green pastures, and distant blue mountains are no printer's dream. Later, hay harvests perfume the countryside.

Montreux, Vevey, and Lausanne, on the Lake of Geneva, are French-speaking towns and centers for excursions to the Vaudois, Valais and Savoy mountains. Near Montreux is the fairy-tale Castle of Chillon, built in the twelfth century. The seat of the Reformation is Geneva, which has a monument to the Reformers. Geneva, watch-making center of the world, is headquarters of the Red Cross. The League of Nations buildings there were taken over in 1946 by the UN for its European headquarters.

The Rhone leaves the lake at Geneva, and the rush of its glacier-green water is exciting to see and hear. In nearby Coppet is Madame de Staël's house, exactly as it was, with eighteenth-century wallpaper and furniture, and in Ferney is Voltaire's house, where thousands came to visit him.

The Mecca of winter-sport lovers is the sixty-mile-long valley called the Engadine. St. Moritz is the most famous ski center, with its Cresta and Suretta runs; nearby are Pontresina and Sils, and Davos, with its Parsenn and Kublis, the only seven-mile run. Klosters, Arosa, and Flims are popular with skiers too. Zermatt is the mountain-climbers' center, with unforgettable views of Monte Rosa, the Matterhorn and Dent Blanche.

South of the St. Gotthard pass is the Ticino, with the lake resorts of Lugano, Locarno and Ascona (where Jung lived), to mention three of the most frequently visited places in this lovely Italian-speaking region of Switzerland.

A tip to gourmets: eat the lovely black cherry jam, the cheese *fondues* with local white wine and, of course, eat and drink the chocolate, which is the best in the world. And wherever you go by railroad in Switzerland you can be sure to get there on time.

SOUTHERN FRANCE

THE man who said "Everyone has two countries, his own and France" has long been forgotten, but the truth of the saying has not and probably never will be. Count Keyserling wrote that France embodies the one universally enjoyable harmony between man and his surroundings that is to be found in Europe. Every bit of France is cultivated, like a garden; the French are cultivated too, charming, civilized, sophisticated, witty. And by nature they are realists, intensely frank, practical and sensibly shrewd, as much so in the south, the part of France visited first in this book, as in the north, to which we shall go at the end of our first, or on our second, trip.

Our trip to southern France begins at Avignon, where in the fourteenth century the Popes lived in pleasant exile, leaving the town a handsome palace. This and the Rhone bridge of nursery-song fame are its two main historic attractions. Roman France remains very much present in many of the splendid local towns and cities, Besançon and Narbonne, for example, Nîmes and Arles. In Nîmes, chief town of the *département* of Gard, there are Roman baths; a temple dedicated to Diana; the *Tour Magne*, which has been called "a dateless tube"; the Maison Carrée; and a well-preserved arena dating back to the time of Augustus. The arena is now used for bullfights.

Arles is also famous for its Roman arena (bullfights are held here too), its amphitheater, originally built to seat nearly 25,000 spectators — and the Alyscamps, a funeral (but not funereal!) avenue. The Pont du Gard, a perfectly preserved Roman three-tiered aqueduct, is nearby. Arles is noted too for its festive folk costumes and the bright pictures Van Gogh painted in and around it, at the end of the last century. Nearby, at Stes.-Maries-de-la-Mer, all the gypsies of Europe gather to honor St. Sara in May and October.

Among the olive groves in mid-Provence is Les Baux, a unique, isolated mass of rock with piles of stones and memories. In the Middle Ages a castle stood here, built by the powerful lords of Baux, an enchanting setting for the songs of troubadours and the flourishing cult of courtly love. But when Les Baux became a Protestant stronghold, King Louis XIII ordered the castle destroyed. The minstrel now is the mistral, the dry, cold wind which blows through the rubble and the crags. Also in Bouches-du-Rhône is charming Aix-en-Provence, which the Romans loved for its warm springs. Aix surely has more fountains per street than any other town its size. It also has an excellent university, founded in 1413, and the lovely Cours Mirabeau, an avenue of plane trees planted in the seventeenth century to replace the town wall. Mont Ste. Victoire looks much like Cézanne's impressions of it, as does the famous artist's little house. Aiguesmortes is a walled city, from which St. Louis sailed to the Crusades.

Lying east of Marseille and stretching all the way to the Italian border is Europe's favorite playground, the Côte d'Azur, with its sunny temperate climate, its fabulous harbors and beaches, its smart shops, clubs, elegant restaurants and cafés. Here as everywhere in France you can wine and dine on the best cooking west of China. Overlooking the shores of the bluest and mildest of waters are Cannes, with its fashionable yacht harbor; Nice, the largest town, where Queen Victoria used to go; Antibes with its sixteenth-century chateau; and Menton, on Italy's border.

Between Nice and Menton lies Monaco, the sovereign principality of the Rainiers, so tiny that it is measured in acres rather than miles. Within its borders is Monte Carlo, with its famous Casino surrounded by luxuriant gardens, hotels and bougan-villaea-draped walls and villas. Monte Carlo's first gambling concession was granted in 1861 and today its annual tribute supports the government as the medieval shipping tax once did.

Behind the coastal resorts lies unspoiled, wonderful mountain country with sunny villages and towns, terraced gardens, vineyards, olive and pine groves, gorges and acres of flowers grown for the flower markets and the perfume factories, one of which can be visited at Grasse. Renoir, Matisse, Dufy, Picasso and other painters lived and live on or near the Riviera, and writers through the years have eulogized it. "I have never seen any scenery that could surpass that which presents itself to the eye on crossing the mountains that lead to Antibes," wrote the charming Countess of Blessington in 1823. "The arbutus, myrtle and jessamine grow in wild profusion at each side of the road... the turf is bedded with wild thyme." And, though today the Corniches and beaches may be crowded, nothing can change the Riviera's chief drawing cards, its natural beauty, its climate, its gaiety.

North of the Riviera is Savoy, which was a separate kingdom until 1860. Here is Megève and here Chamonix, at the foot of Mont Blanc, with its 15,780 foot peak, Europe's highest. Here too is the Mer de Glace, the biggest glacier; the Brévent, where the whole chain can be seen to the best advantage. Grenoble is the key town of the French Alps and a ski and glove center. In the middle of the lower Alps of the Dauphiné is the Grande Chartreuse where, since the Carthusian order was founded in 1084, monks have lived the severest of rules in utter solitude among dense forests and superb mountain peaks.

In France's southwest corner are the provinces of Languedoc and Gascony, with yet more hills and mountains. These lead into the wonderful Basque country. Five fascinating and completely different places to visit in the region are Toulouse, home town of the famous Counts of Toulouse and today one of the most important centers of culture in the south; Bayonne, the largest French town inhabited by the Basques; Biarritz, the expensive beach resort the Empress Eugénie made fashionable; Lourdes, the shrine of Bernadette to which more than a million people make pilgrimage each year; and Carcassonne, the most perfectly restored medieval fortified town in all France, the masterpiece of Viollet-le-Duc. All these lie in the foothills of the Pyrenees, high mountains with excellent skiing and climbing, glaciers and waterfalls, separating yet joining France and Spain.

SPAIN

South of the Pyrenees, how different it is from France! You are either burning hot or bitter cold, and measure, for the French a virtue, is for the Spaniards a vice.

One of the most significant years in Spanish history was 1492, when Columbus found the New World for Ferdinand and Isabella. In Spain the same year ended eight hundred years of Muslim Moorish rule.

The second-largest city in Spain, and a great industrial center, is the Mediterranean port of Barcelona, founded in the third century B.C. and named after Hamilcar Barca, the Carthaginian. It has a fifteenth-century university, a dozen or so museums, and many monuments including the Gothic cathedral, built over the Roman Temple of Jupiter. Cervantes' town house is down by the harbor. The city has a bull ring, of course, good shops and beautiful avenues, flower-filled gardens and parks.

To the north of Barcelona stretches the Costa Brava, the Riviera of Spain, and down the coast, south, is the orange- and lemon-growing country with Valencia at its heart. Fifty minutes east by air from Barcelona are the Balearic Islands — Majorca, where Chopin and George Sand stayed, and Minorca, a short trip east. Both islands offer attractive beaches, comfortable accommodations, and just the right climate.

Northwest from Barcelona is Montserrat, the serrated "holy mountain," with its strange rock formations, the *gistaus* or "stone watchmen." The mountain is inaccessible on three sides, but a road and railroad scramble up on the northeast to the ninth-century Benedictine abbey with its black image of the Virgin attributed to St. Luke. Here St. Ignatius of Loyola laid his sword before the miraculous image and dedicated his new life to the Virgin. At five thousand feet is the hermitage of San Geronimo, and in Manresa St. Ignatius, recovering from the injuries received at the battle of Pamplona, wrote the *Spiritual Exercises* in a cavern below the church which bears his name.

Cordova was the first Roman *colonia* in Spain and later one of the most splendid capitals of the Mohammedan world. It still has Roman remains as well as the huge cathedral, which was once the chief mosque of the Moors. Second only in size to that of Mecca, and the greatest example of Islamic religious art in Europe, the cathedral contains nineteen aisles and nearly nine hundred columns of various styles, some made of marble, some of jasper or porphyry.

The most spectacular of the secular Moorish monuments in all Spain is the Alhambra in Granada, the "Aladdin's palace of delights," as Longfellow called it. The Alhambra was built by the Nasrides family who came to power in 1231 and ruled for two hundred and fifty years. The Court of the Lions, with its famous black marble lions supporting a fountain, was completed by Mohammed V (1334-1391), and the Court of the Myrtles, opening into the palace, was finished by Yusef I. The 5,000 honeycomb cells in the dome of the Hall of the Two Sisters, and the lacy reliefs of the Mirador de Daraxa represent Islamic ornamental art at its very best. The Generalife, the Moorish summer residence on the hill dominating the Alhambra, is a series of airy courtyards and galleries opening on to unbelievably beautiful terraced gardens and fountains. Granada is the city where Washington Irving lived and wrote, and where, in the Cathedral, the unifiers of Spain — Ferdinand and Isabella — lie buried. On the Sacre Monte Hill, outside the city, over two thousand gypsies live in caves. These *gitanes*, who dance magnificently, proudly trace their ancestry to the pharaohs of Egypt.

The best time to go to Seville is for the *feria* in Easter Week, when the whole city turns out in dazzlingly colorful costume for the religious festivals, followed by bullfighting and spirited flamenco dancing. In the fifteenth-century cathedral — the biggest in Christendom after Rome — the Dance of the Boys is performed in costumes of Philip III's time in front of the high altar, and spectacular processions weave through the city streets. The Alcazar, fortress and residence of the Sultans, La Giralda, the gigantic twelfth-century minaret, and the Duke of Alba's *casa*

must be seen; so too should the Fine Arts Museum with its paintings by Murillo, who, like the great Velazquez, was born in Seville.

Malaga, a Phoenician port, lying in one of the most fertile parts of Spain, is a delightful Mediterranean resort with a fine cathedral and a Moorish castle. Cadiz, a Visigothic and later Moorish sea town, was the scene of many battles and the home port of the great Armada. It is also the city where Murillo died and Manuel de Falla was born.

Toledo, city of steel and the Inquisition, remains much as El Greco painted it in his View of Toledo, one version of which hangs in the Metropolitan Museum in New York. The winding Tagus, the hill, and cathedral are there and the clusters of houses which show little change except in number. One of El Greco's greatest paintings, *The Burial of Count Orgaz*, is in the church of Santo Tomé; others hang in the art museum. In Toledo too are the Santa Cruz hospital, with its lovely courtyard; the exquisite El Cristo de la Luz, a former mosque built in 922; and Santa Maria la Blanca, which was founded as a synagogue in the twelfth century and became a church in 1405. Toledo, for centuries a center of Arab and Jewish culture, was, and is, also famous for its steel blades and gun barrels.

Avila, fifty-five miles west of Madrid, is an austere, walled city standing four thousand feet high on a flat ridge in the sierras. Nine gates, eighty-eight towers, and the massive granite walls are perfectly preserved. The cathedral, looking more like a fortress than a place of worship, contains a monument to St. Teresa. Her words "I need no rest, what I need is crosses," and her subsequent prayers and deeds demonstrated Teresa's mettle; a convent is built on the site where she was born. No one can contemplate Avila without thinking of St. Teresa any more than one can visit Burgos without thinking of El Cid.

Madrid, the youngest and largest of Spain's great cities and the highest of Europe's capitals, has largely been rebuilt since the Civil War (1936-1939). It abounds in modern buildings and has the lovely El Retiro park with a lake. In the Plaza de España are the Cervantes memorial and bronze statues of Don Quixote and Sancho Panza. But the real pride of Madrid is the Prado, one of the great museums of the world. A fabulous collection of Goyas, a roomful of El Grecos, many Titians and over forty magnificent paintings by Velazquez, are among the masterpieces on view here. Most of the paintings came from the collections of Charles V and Philip II. The finest monuments to Goya's art are the glorious church frescoes which decorate the cupola and all the niches and corners of San Antonio de la Florida. Outside Madrid is Aranjuez, with its eighteenth-century palace, donated by General Franco to young Prince Juan Carlo and his Greek bride. Thirty miles from Madrid, on the southern slopes of the Sierra de Guadarrama mountains, is the Escorial, Philip II's palace-monastery. This is in Spanish Baroque style, but with a unique ground plan representing the shape of the gridiron on which St. Lawrence, to whom Philip dedicated the palace, was martyred. The church in the Escorial is one of the finest Renaissance buildings of Europe, and in the library and gallery of the palace are rare manuscripts and great paintings, including El Greco's *Martyrdom of St. Maurice* and the *Hay Wain* of Hieronymus Bosch.

To the visitor Spain offers Mediterranean and Moorish architecture and art, mountains, valleys and sunny beaches, music, dancing and bullfights — all these and more, can be enjoyed at a surprisingly small cost.

PORTUGAL

THE capital of this "unitary and corporative republic" lying between Spain and the Atlantic is the city of Lisbon. Like Rome, Lisbon is built on seven hills; piled high on and against these hills are houses, church towers, and office buildings supporting a sea of tiled roofs. Here and there interrupting slants and squares of greenery denote a garden or park.

The *ascensoies* will save your breath as you go up and down the steep hills to see the magnificent views and landmarks. These are many. From the Casa de los Bucos, crowning the city, can be seen one of the best panoramas of Lisbon, the river Tagus and the sea. Built on the Tagus itself in the early sixteenth century to defend it, is the Belem Tower — in Manueline style, which is a cross between Gothic and Moorish. Of earlier date is the twelfth-century Sé Patriarcal, a mosque before the 1755 earthquake laid most of it in ruins. Famous too is the fifteenth-century Jeronimos Monastery and Church, whose cloisters and gateway, built by the great architect João de Castilho, survived the earthquake. Here lie buried Vasco da Gama, first to find a sea route around Africa to India; the national poet Luiz Vaz de Camoëns; and, in the famous stone elephant-borne tombs, many Kings and Queens of Portugal.

Other sights in and around Lisbon include the Black Horse Square, surrounded by classic buildings; Queluz, the enchanting small copy of Versailles built by King John V; the eighteenth-century Aqueducto das Aguas Livres, which still brings water to the city over thirty-five high arches; the fish market, where many of the natives dress in tartan-plaid costumes; the mosaic-paved esplanades and squares, the fashionable Avenida da Liberdade, and everywhere gay-colored houses warmed by the sun. "It would be hard indeed to exaggerate the beauty of Lisbon," wrote Sacheverell Sitwell, "... a city where, although the trams run late and early, and motor traffic never ceases, you are wakened by a cock crowing in some hidden backyard or corner of a garden, and standing in the window you look down at the bank of geraniums in front of the house opposite and they are glowing, in incandescence, like bluish flowers, for the dawn has not reached to them... and looking up are the roofs the morning just touches, that moment, on the white walls of a castle, high up, the Castelo da São Jorge, like a celestial city in a cloudless sky."

On the coast fifteen miles west of Lisbon is fashionable Estoril, a resort with good year-round climate, good hotels, good food and a casino. A short drive from it is the lovely town of Sintra, Lord Byron's "little Eden," with beautiful gardens and paths. All around are eucalyptus and cork trees, magnolias, camellias, cinerarias and countless other flowers that flourish in the warm climate. Of local interest are the ruined Moorish castle and the Palacio da Sintra, with dazzling mosaics, a beautiful garden, and fountains. And overlooking the sea on the rocky hill of Peña close by is the castle built by Prince Ferdinand of Saxe-Coburg-Gotha in 1840. Between Leiria, another town with a castle, and the ocean, are the handsome pine woods planted by King Denis in the early fourteenth century.

Fatima, a hundred miles north of Lisbon, is a comparatively new shrine where twice a year pilgrims honor the little shepherds Francisco, Lucia and Jacinta, whose story of their vision no one at first would believe. And you should go to the coast again to see the little fishing villages and towns such as Nazaré, where you can watch the colorful ships and fishermen and the tiled market squares.

Farther north is the city of Coimbra, which was Moorish until Ferdinand I and El Cid captured it in 1064, just two years before the Normans invaded England. Coimbra was Portugal's capital until 1260. Its university, one of the oldest in Europe, is where Camoëns studied, and the *Fonte dos Amores*, Coimbra's beautiful park, is where Dom Pedro's beloved Inés de Castro was stabbed in 1355. The Machado de Castro Museum in the old Episcopal Palace displays excellent ecclesiastic art, largely of local origin.

Still farther north are the Douro valley and Oporto, the second largest of Portugal's cities. Here are attractive Roman, Gothic and baroque churches and cathedrals. Here also are the Soares dos Reio Museum (the old Royal Palace) containing masterpieces from the Middle Ages, and two bridges spanning the Douro, one of them designed by Eiffel of Paris. In Oporto the old mixes with the new and in the bustling city's narrow streets donkey and ox-carts jog along beside the noisy cars and buses.

In the mountain country around are the vineyards from which Oporto has made its fortune — giving its name to the only authentic Port wine in the world. At vintage time, in the hot green valley, laborers fill their wicker baskets and carry them strapped to their foreheads, to the *quntas*, where, as the vats begin to fill, barefoot vintagers tread the grapes to slow, rhythmic music played by a musician on a concertina or guitar. "The grandeur of the upper Douro can only be described as biblical" writes Yves Bottineau, and "if there be indeed a chosen people its Promised Land would be on the slopes of this valley. It is one of the pleasantest districts in all Portugal, surpassing all others in its noble blend of the bounty of nature with the handiwork of man."

NORTHERN EUROPE

IRELAND

THIRTY spokes has a wheel, but it is the space between the spokes that makes it a wheel, says the Chinese Tao. Similarly, Europe has many countries, but it is the sea around them that makes most of them what they are. This is especially true of Ireland. The Republic covers 27,137 square miles of the island's total of 32,500, with three million people, and its beauty is, as Stephen Gwynn says, above all the beauty of waters. "The sea to begin with... then the fresh water. Ireland is above all the land of lakes (there are around eight hundred). And wherever a man is, wherever he is brought up in Ireland, he has some river to fall in love with." Cynics would add, wherever a man is there is the rain, that raineth every day, and gives the women their lovely complexions and the country its green, green color.

Ireland became Christian before 500 A.D., and from the sixth to the eighth centuries produced a flowering of art and knowledge. Irish monks brought Christianity to northern Europe, and Greek back to it. And Ireland produced such masterpieces as the Celtic crosses, of which seven still remain.

Tara, once the religious, political and cultural center, with a king's palace, has nothing left but three fields full of mounds; Kells, where the famous Book was illuminated in the sixth century, has the ruins of a monastery founded by St. Columba. Blarney Castle, with its kissing stone, as great an attraction as ever, is in charming countryside five miles from Cork; and Cashel, with Cormac's chapel, a cross to St. Patrick who visited there in 450, a round tower, and a roofless cathedral high on its great rock, is in Tipperary. The Cathedral was burned down in 1496 by the Earl of Kildare, who excused himself afterward to Henry VII, saying, "I thought the archbishop was inside."

Most roads lead to Dublin, which is largely an eighteenth-century city, but founded on a prehistoric Celtic site. Much has been restored—St. Patrick's

Cathedral and Christ Church in the nineteenth century through the munificence of distillers, the Four Courts as recently as 1926 after the fighting of 1921. Trinity College, the eighteenth-century Custom House, designed (as the Four Courts were) by Tamer Ganda; Dublin Castle, dating back to the thirteenth century; and Phoenix Park, all 1760 acres of it, are among the best sights to see. The Lane Collection in the National Gallery is excellent, as are the two theaters, the Abbey and the Gate. Plays by J. M. Synge and Sean O'Casey were first given here, and still are, but Dublin is most of all James Joyce's city, and readers of *Ulysses* can follow Bloom around there from dawn to midnight.

Irish whisky is wonderful: the stout tamer but splendid. *Barmbrac*, a rich bread, is also to be highly recommended. Irish linens and Irish tweed are world-famous.

So, too, is the countryside, from Londonderry to Tipperary, from Kildare to Limerick, with white-washed, thatch-roofed farmsteads and a patchwork of cultivated fields, grassland and woods. The country is lovely, as are Ireland's dancing, singing, poetic, tall-tale-telling people.

SCOTLAND

THE best scenery in Scotland is in the west; the best buildings are in the east. Gaelic is still spoken in the west and in the Hebrides, Mull, the Orkneys, Shetlands, Skye and other islands. The Scots thrive on oatmeal, which prompted Dr. Johnson's remark, "that Oats in England are the food of horses, in Scotland of men." They also thrive on herrings, "bloaters" and "kippers," on whisky, scones, shortbread and haggis (sheep's stomach). Scotland offers superlative golf, fishing, deer-stalking, grouse-shooting, sailing, and its own special sport, curling on ice.

Christianity came to Scotland from Ireland early. St. Ninian's Candida Casa was built in 435 and St. Columba landed in Iona in 563. Dr. Johnson, kinder to monuments than to oatmeal, noted "That man is little to be envied whose piety would not grow warmer in the ruins of Iona." A little over three miles long and one mile wide, Iona has a cathedral dating from 1204, St. Oran's twelfth-century chapel, and two crosses surviving of the three hundred and sixty the island once possessed.

Edinburgh, set on Castle Hill, has been called the Northern Athens. The Castle itself is tremendously effective, surrounded on three sides by precipices with a magnificent view of the city, the Firth of Forth, the Fifeshire coast and Pentland Hills. Military ceremonies are held here "with all the pomp of swirling kilts and martial bagpipes." Princes Street, with Robert Adam's Register House, its monument to Walter Scott and fine shops, is the handsomest street in all Scotland. Edinburgh's National War Memorial has modern stained-glass windows by Douglas Strachan. A walk along High Street will take you past the much-restored St. Giles Cathedral and John Knox's house to Holyrood Palace, the Queen's official residence in Scotland. Holyrood is full of memories of the Queen's ancestress, the tragic Mary Stuart. Queen Mary's bedroom, Darnley's apartments, the room where Rizzio was murdered, all are on view. Falkland Palace, Stirling Castle and Leven Castle each recall Mary too. Edinburgh's sixteenth-century university is an especially fine one; and the city's Festival of Music and Dramatic Art is attended by people from all over the world.

Glasgow, with its industrial suburbs, is not pretty, but the city is the gateway to the wild and rugged

West Highlands. The Trossachs, written about by Scott in *Rob Roy* and *The Lady of the Lake*; Loch Lomond, the biggest of the lakes; Ben Nevis, rising nearly five thousand feet, the highest mountain in the British Isles; Loch Ness, famed for its mysterious monster, less seen and heard about these days; Inveraray Castle; Oban, with its Highland Gatherings; the Macleod's Dunvegan on Skye, the oldest inhabited castle in Great Britain; Glenfinnan, where a monument commemorates Bonnie Prince Charlie; Glencoe, the grim pass where the Campbells massacred their hosts the Macdonalds (a deed that has never been wholly forgiven and will never be forgotten); the Caledonian Canal, with Forts William and Augustus; nearby Elgin Cathedral and Cawdor Castle that recall Macbeth and Macduff — all can easily be reached from Glasgow.

Aberdeen, granite city of jokes and center of the whitefishing industry; Perth, once a Roman settlement; and Dundee, the city of linen, jute, shortcake and marmalade, all have lovely surrounding country. Along Deeside is Balmoral Castle, near Braemar, where the famous annual Highland Gathering or Games is held. The mile-long Forth Bridge, with two seventeen-hundred-foot spans, built by Sir John Fowler and Sir Benjamin Baker in 1883-1890, and the Finnan Viaduct should be seen too. Twelve miles from Dundee is St. Andrews, university town and seaport with four golf courses, the most famous in the world.

The border country, south of Edinburgh, is full of castles. Three of the finest are Drumlanrig Castle, built in the seventeenth century by Sir William Bruce, who redesigned Holyrood Palace; Blackven Castle; and Robert Adam's Castle in Ayrshire. There are many abbeys too, among them Melrose Abbey near Abbotsford, the home of Walter Scott, who wrote lovingly of its "slender shafts of shapely stone"; Dryburgh Abbey, where Scott lies buried; and Jedburgh Abbey.

Highland dress with its kilts and tartans is legendary and still much worn. Scottish bagpipes are movingly beautiful. Scotch mist and heather-covered moors, large lakes and craggy mountain passes, green valleys and flock after flock of sheep, all add to the completeness of the picture of Scotland.

ENGLAND

No doubt the same flesh and blood covers all bones, but, as Humpty Dumpty said to Alice, how different are people's faces. And what could be more English than cricket or Eton, or tea and crumpets, or driving on the opposite side of the road from almost everyone else in the world? The clipped English accent is an everyday reality; so too the leisureliness of the Englishman, his knack for understatement, and his obsession with words, which he pronounces not at all the way they are spelled. Where but here would Cholmondeley be pronounced "Chumley" or Uttoxeter "Uxtah," and where but here would you encounter places with names like Giggleswick, Pinfarthing, Lower Slaughter, Rime Intrinseca, or, indeed, Wormwood Scrubs?

After sticking his neck out in London to catch a glimpse of royalty, the visitor goes on to visit Shakespeare's birthplace and Canterbury Cathedral, and then at Stonehenge on Salisbury plain he will see what men "driven by fear of Power invisible" did with stone before recorded time.

The insides of England are as English and special as the outsides. Today most of the great houses, such as the Duke of Bedford's Woburn Abbey, with a private zoo, are open to the public for half a crown. Beaulieu and Wilton in Wiltshire, Knole with its three hundred and sixty-five rooms in Kent, and many others, were sites of abbeys until the Reformation, when Henry VIII gave them away — Wilton to his brother-in-law William Herbert, whose descendants have owned it ever since. Holbein designed Wilton's porch, Inigo Jones, Van Dyke, and others the towers and chambers, Palladio the bridge across the river.

The South of England from Kent, Surrey, and Sussex in the East to the less crowded area that history and Hardy called Wessex, has some of the prettiest houses, villages and towns in the country, as well as the mildest climate. The New Forest is near Southampton, where the *Queens* dock. To the east is Sussex with its Cinque Ports; Rye, one of the five, has charming buildings and cobbled streets which Henry James loved. Winchelsea, with good modern stained glass in the church, some think even prettier. In Sussex too is the charming village of Petworth with its manor, housing a wonderful collection of old masters and Grinling Gibbons carvings.

On the south coast are the big seaside resorts with piers; Brighton, "London by the Sea," with its pavilion; Eastbourne with Hurstmonceaux Castle, and the famous girls' school, Roedean, both nearby; and Bournemouth, with its Branksome Pines and lovely rhododendrons. A few miles north of Eastbourne is Lewes, a castled county town and stopping-off place for Glyndebourne where the summer music festival takes place — evening dress obligatory — in an opera house surrounded by a garden, where the flowers and food are fine.

In Wiltshire is Lacock, with its many-chimneyed abbey, and Bath, the *Aquae Solis* of the Romans, in whose baths one can still swim the year round in naturally warm spring water. Bath was transformed in the eighteenth century by John Wood and his son from a small provincial watering place into a second Pompeii. Prior Park, Ralph Allen's Palladian house (where Alexander Pope and William Pitt loved

to visit), Queen's Square, Royal Crescent and Marlborough Buildings are all wonderful examples of Palladian architecture. Pultenay Bridge, built in 1770 by Robert Adams, is covered and contains built-in shops. Nearby is Wells, visited for the west front of its cathedral and its "close" with pond and swans.

Salisbury Cathedral, the first in early English, or Pointed, style, was the subject of one of Constable's most popular paintings. In Devon, famous for clotted cream, are Welcombe in the north, with the old church dedicated to St. Necton the martyr, who had his head cut off and afterward carried it; and quaint Clovelly, an artists' resort. Near Torquay on the south coast is Brixham, an attractive fishery and boat center, and around Prawle Point lies Plymouth, where Drake set off to destroy the Armada. St. Ives of riddle fame and Penzance, home port of Gilbert and Sullivan's pirates, are in Cornwall, whose rugged coastline has picturesque harbors and villages, lovely beaches and views.

There is no pleasanter way of seeing the country than driving around it to go old-house and castle-visiting. This will take you through historic towns and many of England's thirteen thousand villages, some particularly famed for their beauty, such as Castle Combe, Winsford, Chilham, Lavenham, and Coggeshall.

A tour into the heart of England could start at Windsor. Overlooking the ancient forest is the huge Castle, started by William the Conqueror, added to mostly by Henry III and Edward III, and lived in part of the year by Her Majesty as by all English monarchs before her. The castle has a magnificent library and one of the greatest collections of drawings in the world, especially of Leonardo da Vinci and other Italian masters. Here too is St. George's chapel, with its glorious roof and stained-glass windows. In the town of Windsor are the houses of Jane Seymour, who escaped the fate of Henry VIII's other wives by dying in time, and of Nell Gwyn, the brilliant, witty actress loved by everyone, especially Charles II.

Opposite Windsor is Eton, largest of the ancient English public schools, founded by Henry VI in 1440-1441, with playing fields and lovely buildings that mellow even the thousand teen-agers attending it. From Eton a drive of about forty miles up the Thames will take you through Maidenhead and Henley, where the regattas are held, to Oxford. The university dates back to the twelfth century and has some thirty colleges, of which Christ Church (called "The House" from part of its Latin name, *Aedes Christi*), founded in 1525 by Cardinal Wolsey; New College; Balliol; and Magdalen (which you must pronounce "Maudlin" or no one will understand you) with its tower, at the top of which boys still sing at dawn on May morning, are the "top" four. The public buildings at Oxford include the Bodleian Library, the Ashmolean Museum, Christopher Wren's Sheldonian Theatre, and the pre-Reformation university chapel, Saint Mary the Virgin. The view from the dome of the Radcliffe Camera is famous.

Between Oxford and Stratford are the rolling Cotswold hills, with stone cottages, houses, and manors snuggled in their folds. Here are Minster Lovell; Burford lolloping down its hill, with every house a gem; Lechlade; Fairford; Quenington; and Broadway — perhaps the most enchanting of all. Stratford-upon-Avon in Warwickshire is so wonderfully preserved that it is still a joy to visit the famous houses and the Memorial Theatre, where Shakespeare's plays are given from March to November.

Within a forty-mile radius of Stratford are places where great battles were fought — Worcester (now better known for its cathedral and the sauce named after it), Tewkesbury, and Bosworth.

In Cheshire on the border of Wales is Chester, a quaint old town with Roman remains, half-timbered houses, and unique streets lined with two-storied, shop-filled arcades called "rows." From here a tour through Wales could include Conway and Caernarvon castles, both built by Edward I; Caernarvon was the castle from which his son was proclaimed Prince of Wales. In Wales is Llangollen, headquarters for the annual Eisteddfod, or song festival of local and international competing choirs. The Welsh mountain scenery is magnificent and the highest peak here is Snowdon.

North from Chester through industrial Lancashire is the Lake District. Here among the hills and mountains are Derwentwater and many other poet-sung lakes, streams, and ponds visited by Wordsworth, Coleridge, Southey and others.

On England's east coast is Yorkshire, the largest county, with many industrial cities. York, the capital, has a splendid cathedral with the "seven sisters" windows and some lovely old streets. Here too are seacoast resorts and the moors made famous in Emily Brontë's *Wuthering Heights*. To the south lies Lincolnshire, most of it flat, with the fen district of Hereward the Wake, and acres and acres of fertile land used for bulb-growing, farming, and market gardening. At Lincoln is another of the great English cathedrals. Norfolk is especially enjoyed for sailing on the "Broads", Suffolk for its pretty countryside, which Constable loved to paint, and Cambridge for its magnificent university with King's College Chapel, one of the most beautiful in the world. Nearby is Ely, with yet another magnificent cathedral. Essex, just north of London, is noted for its seed-growing industry, Tiptree jams, and lovely old houses, near the marshland to which Paul Gallico's "Snow Goose" flew.

A "first" look at London usually starts off with the houses of Parliament, Big Ben and Westminster Abbey; then Downing Street, where the Prime Minister lives at Number 10, the horseguards, the Cenotaph, and Trafalgar Square with Nelson's column and the pigeon-favoured lions. Here are the National Gallery, with its great collection of old and modern masters, the National Portrait Gallery, and the statue of King Charles I. At the end of the Mall is Buckingham Palace, where Christopher Robin went with Alice to watch the changing of the guard, a daily ritual.

London is the best place in the world for theaters. The standard of acting is the highest, and you can get tickets without booking weeks in advance, at a very reasonable price.

Before leaving London, see the Christopher Wren churches, including St. Paul's; visit the Tower of London, with its horrific reminders of rack and rope and headman's axe, and the Law Courts and British Museum. Take a walk up fashionable Bond Street, with its art galleries and specialty shops, and along Regent Street and Piccadilly, all in the heart of London's West End. The parks and gardens are lovely, too: St. James's Park, Hyde Park, Kensington Gardens, Regent's Park with its huge zoo, and Kew with its magnificent botanical gardens.

London has everything, including excellent food: English at Rules or Simpson's; various foreign kinds in Soho; Chinese in South Kensington; Indian around Oxford Circus. It's the friendliest of all big cities and the police are the politest in the world.

NORWAY

MOST of Norway is rugged country of extreme grandeur, "of vast panoramas and of small but significant details, from the lonely tree far out on the tundra to the solitary flower in an ocean of heather," as Terje Stigen wrote. Forests occupy twenty-four per cent of the more than 17,000 square miles of land, and the swift rivers are used for floating timber to the mills and for Norway's ambitious hydro-electric power schemes. The Norsk Hydro, for example, produces over a million tons of nitrate fertilizers a year, made from ammonia extracted from air and water.

Norwegians are great travelers; in the twelfth century Sigurd Jorsalfar rode into Constantinople, and in the twentieth century Thor Heyerdahl amazed the world by traveling on a raft 4300 miles across the South Pacific to show that the Polynesian Islands could have been settled from Peru.

Oslo, Norway's capital, celebrated its nine hundredth anniversary in 1950 and was the site of the winter Olympics of 1952. The city was founded by King Harald Haardraade and reached its first heyday around 1300 when the Akershus Fortress was built. The castle was rebuilt in the seventeenth century by King Christian IV of Denmark; from it there is a wonderful view of the harbor, of the city's old and modern architecture, and of the distant wooded hills. Today Oslo is the home port for half the Norwegian merchant fleet, the third largest in the world. Henrik Ibsen, Björnstjerne Björnson, and Sigrid Undset all lived here. Frogner Park is famous for Gustav Vigeland's controversial "sculptural layout" which consists of one hundred and fifty large organic groups. Also to be visited are the University of Oslo; the Royal Palace with its guards; the National Theater, which offers classical drama and an Ibsen cycle; and the Nobel Institute, where the Nobel peace prize is awarded. A quarter of an hour by car from the center of town is the Bygdoy Peninsula, with its superb Folk Museum containing old Norwegian buildings, Viking ships, and Thor Heyerdahl's *Kon-Tiki* raft. Near the city, too, beaches provide excellent swimming in summer and the hills good slopes for skiing in winter.

The magnificent fjords are Norway's unique glory, and when the first orchards blossom along the waterfronts the effect is breathtaking. The fjords fringe the whole western shoreline; many are a mile deep, with walls a mile high. You can take coastal steamer trips to see them or go by car from Stavanger and board one of the local ferries. The Hardanger and the Sogne offer vast expanses of water combined with mountains and glaciers; the Stor and the Geiranger (notable for its sheer cliffs and numerous waterfalls), are among the most spectacular fjords. Of the mountain peaks, the Glittertind and Galdhöpiggen, both over eight thousand feet, are Norway's highest. Three large lakes are Bygdin, Tyin, and Gjende, the latter with its remarkable green water and the high ridge (separating it from Lake Russvatn) along which Ibsen's Peer Gynt rode on the back of a reindeer. The Jostedalsbreen, with glaciers running from it, is Europe's greatest ice-field.

Bergen, birthplace of the composer Edvard Grieg, is Norway's second-largest city, and its fishing center. The harbor and fish market is one of the most colorful and bustling sights in the country. The Hanseatic Museum dates back to when Bergen was one of the greatest of the Hanseatic League towns; the twelfth-century Maria Kirke and the Cathedral are interesting too, but even more so are the fascinating pagoda-like stave churches near Bergen, built of massive timbers and wholly covered with small pointed shingles. This architecture is uniquely Scandinavian. The most famous example of all is the stave church at Borgund, built in the thirteenth century. Trondheim, the principal city of north-central Norway, has a splendid eleventh-century church, a famous technical school, and four lovely bridges crossing the Nid. Trondheim offers good sports and is the gateway to northern Norway, where the midnight sun is visible from May 16 to July 29.

Nearly everywhere in Norway there is wonderful skiing, but the best of all is at Lillehammer, four hours by train from Oslo, where champions come from all over the world. And nearly everywhere there are good hiking, mountain climbing, fishing, sailing, skating, bobsledding, and game-bird shooting. Tourist accommodations are usually simple and good. Norwegians probably have more physical energy than any other people; they work hard, play hard and eat extremely well. Culturally, they lean toward England, as the Danes do toward France and the Swedes toward Germany.

SWEDEN

Sweden has integrated industry with the good life; its cities are happy mixtures of ancient and modern. The country has no slums, no illiteracy, no poverty, and it has the highest level of social security imaginable. Its craftsmanship in silver, steel, glass, iron, china, wood, or textiles is in excellent modern taste and is admirably functional. Nothing Swedes make is ugly, shoddy or amateurish.

Of Sweden's 173,349 square miles, fifty per cent is covered by forests, thirty per cent by mountains, and ten per cent by lakes. In Sweden, which forms the eastern part of the Scandinavian peninsula, nearly seven and a half million people live at peace with the world. Stockholm, on the Baltic, is a beautiful city, airy, spacious, and luminous, with light reflected in its surrounding waters. The modern Town Hall, with its square red brick tower handsomely topped with three golden crowns, the Norrebro bridge, the Storkyrka, or Great Church, founded by Birger Jarl in 1264, the Riddarholm Church, where Sweden's Kings and Queens are buried, the Riddarhus (House of Nobles) established in Queen Christina's reign, and the Royal Palace, open to the public — all are Stockholm landmarks. The garden of the famous sculptor Carl Milles, the National Museum, and the theaters too should be visited. Sweden's Royal Dramatic Theater has produced such international stars as Greta Garbo and Ingrid Bergman, and besides plays of native origin the dozen or so legitimate theaters offer new shows from New York and European capitals. In Stockholm the Nobel prizes are distributed annually, and here Ingmar Bergman plans his macabre masterpieces.

Drottningholm, the King's lovely island summer palace on Lake Mälaren, is less than an hour by boat from Stockholm. Drottningholm was built in the seventeenth century by Nicodemus Tessin; it has a Chinese pagoda and a theater, established in 1759, where plays are given every summer in the original costumes and with the original stage machinery. Three hours by boat from Stockholm is Gripsholm palace — built in 1537 by Gustavus Vasa. The palace has four red towers, overlooking Lake Malaren, which serves it as a moat. In the building there is a large and wonderful portrait collection.

Uppsala, university town, about forty miles north of Stockholm, is the seat of the Archbishop and has a cathedral dating back to 1287, restored in the 1890s, and containing a manuscript of the Gospels translated by Bishop Ulfilas in the fourth century. It was in Uppsala that Swedenborg refused the chair of mathematics; here Queen Christina abdicated, and here the great Secretary-General of the United Nations, Dag Hammarskjold, lies buried.

Dalecarlia, generally referred to as the heart of Sweden, is the oldest industrial center, and a beautiful resort region besides. Lake Siljan is surrounded by attractive villages and woodland. The sight of the sun catching at the trunks of the beeches which streak the forests with silver is unforgettable. At the midsummer festivals natives dress in folk costumes, play music and dance under the midnight sun. In winter Dalecarlia is cloaked in snow, and the fifty-five mile Vasa ski race is run every year.

The island of Gotland is the largest in the Baltic, with Visby, a member of the Hanseatic League until 1293, its lovely capital, situated on an old trade route via Novgorod to Asia. With its ancient town walls, crumbling ruins and flowers, Visby is fondly and aptly called the "town of ruins and roses."

In Sweden's south is the richest and most thickly populated province, Malmöhus. There are no mountains to look up at here; instead, attractive hills roll from farmland to farmland and from castle to castle. Here are Vittskovle, Gofdeborg, Glimningehus, Rotneros — each castle a gem. Malmö, the province's capital, is a modern city with sprinklings of Renaissance architecture, while Lund, once an archbishopric and still a university town, has wholly preserved its delightfully medieval character.

All regions in Sweden are easily reached by road, boat or rail. " Sunlit Nights Land Cruises " will take you by train as far as the Arctic Circle and back, with sights of the Lapps, their land and their reindeer herds. Everywhere in Sweden accommodations are plentiful, clean and reasonable. Swedish baths are an experience, and the smörgåsbord, of course, is the very best in the world.

FINLAND

THE fifth largest country in Europe, with more woods and lakes to its size than any country in the world, Finland occupies 130,165 square miles and has a population of nearly four and a half million people. It became independent in 1917. Finland's chief export is wood, in the form of both lumber and finished products.

Helsinki, the country's capital, is over four hundred years old, though most of what we see here today has been built in the present century. The modern architecture is exceptionally well designed, as are the parks and squares containing monuments and figures created by Finnish sculptors. The 1952 Olympics were held in Helsinki's Stadium. This should be visited, and so should the five harbors, the Helsinki Zoo, which is reached by ferry, on Koreasaari Island, the Parliament building (open to the public the first Sunday of each month), the City Hall, the Cathedral, and the President's Palace on Market Square. From here boat trips go to the attractive Suomenlinna Islands. Helsinki's shops are modern, and the city boasts the two largest bookshops in the world.

Tampere, Finland's second-largest city, can be reached by motor and water-bus from Helsinki, or by train. The Tammerkoski rapids which flow through Tampere are an extraordinary sight, as is the view from atop the Pyynikki ridge which takes in the whole city and a panorama of the lake country around.

Finland's arts and crafts are in excellent and simple taste, from the traditional to the modern, as can be seen from examples in the Provincial Museum and in shops at Tampere, as well as in Helsinki and other centers. Tampere also boasts two museums featuring modern Finnish art.

From Tampere a water-bus trip to Aulanko will take you through typical Finnish country, "where the play of light on water is strange and more beautiful than in any other region of the globe," as Doré Ogrizek wrote. Aulanko is a wonderful resort with a spectacular national park and the famous Aulanko Hotel with its bathing beaches, tennis courts and sauna (Finnish bath). Visit the fascinating old Hattula church built in 1250, and the thirteenth-century castle, even older than St. Olaf's at Savonlinna. Facing Aulanko across Lake Vanajavesi is Hämeenlinna, the birthplace of the great Finnish composer Jean Sibelius.

In the far north of Finland is Lapland, which casts a spell on all those who go there. "He who goes is compelled to return, and when he goes a second time he may stay, and if he doesn't he'll turn into a reindeer." Visit it once in winter to enjoy the marvelous skiing, and the reindeer-jöring in a one-seated pulka.

DENMARK

DENMARK consists of Jutland, a peninsula, and some five hundred islands, only a hundred of which are inhabited. Sixty per cent of the four-and-a-half-million population live in the towns, yet Denmark produces four times as much food as it needs. The surplus, mostly dairy food, is exported. The mild Danish climate and long coastline provide marvelous swimming and sailing in the summer.

This is the oldest monarchy in Europe, Gorm the Old (born about 883) being the first Danish king. The present monarch lives in Copenhagen's beautiful Amalienborg Palace, where the colorful ceremony of the changing of the guard takes place at noon. The city of Copenhagen was founded by Bishop Absalon in 1167; today it is one of the gayest capitals in northern Europe and one of its busiest ports. The Town Hall Square, dominated by a 350-foot spire, is linked by five narrow mile-long streets collectively called Main Street. The 1640 Stock Exchange is lovely, and the Round Tower distinguished for its fascinating carriage ramp used instead of a staircase. Amalienborg Square, enclosed by four almost identical rococo palaces, built between 1750 and 1760, is one of the most perfect architectural units anywhere. Reflecting Copenhagen's handsome buildings, both medieval and modern, are the numerous canals, whose purpose is to bring the sea close (not, as in Holland, to keep it far away). Motor boats can be hired at moderate cost for a canal-view tour of the entire city.

Copenhagen's Christiansborg Palace, restored in 1928, has a prehistoric section showing the Viking era. Interesting too are the seventeenth-century Rosenborg Palace, where the crown jewels are displayed; the Kunstindustrimuseet, which has exhibits of the arts and crafts of Denmark, and the wonderful museum of musical instruments; the State Museum of Art, containing Danish masters; the Thorvaldsen Museum, with works by that Danish sculptor (1768-1844); and the Arsenal, filled with historic arms and armor.

Other landmarks in Copenhagen are the old Cathedral, with Thorvaldsen's sculptured Apostles and Christ; Langelinie, Copenhagen's favorite promenade, with Hans Andersen's Little Mermaid sculptured in bronze by Erichsen; and the twenty-acre Tivoli Gardens, laid out in 1843 and beautifully kept today as a public park.

There are still over two thousand great private estates in Denmark, some of them royal palaces like Fredensborg, where the Royal Family goes in the autumn. You should certainly see Liselund, a miniature French château built in 1792 by a French banker after he had escaped the revolution; Frede-riksborg Palace, now the National Historical Museum, built on three small islands on a lake in the early seventeenth century; and Kronborg Castle at Elsinore, built by King Frederick II in the sixteenth century and the setting today for summer performances of *Hamlet* in the courtyard.

Only a few miles from Copenhagen is Odense, to which St. Canute's shrine drew thousands of pilgrims in the Middle Ages. Odense, provincial capital in the heart of "the fairy island of Fyn," is Hans Christian Andersen's town, and among its many delightful old houses is the one in which Andersen was born, now a museum. Across the island and in the midst of farmland is the interesting old walled town of Faaborg, with its castle.

The second-largest city and seaport in Denmark is Aarhus, the capital of Jutland. Aarhus has an ultramodern Town Hall, an open-air museum, and a Gothic Cathedral dating from 1201. Like Copenhagen, which can be reached by boat, train or bus, Aarhus has a gay night life and splendid accommodations and food. From it excursions can be taken to the lovely lake districts around Silkeborg.

While in Denmark take a "life-seeing" tour, featuring the modern social-welfare institutions, schools, old people's homes, hospitals, modern farms and engineering triumphs such as Europe's longest bridge, the Storstrom. Then you will agree with Hamlet that, at least in Denmark, man is a piece of work indeed.

BELGIUM

CULTURALLY, the Low Countries are a Germano-Latin frontier. Belgium emphasizes the Latin, Holland the German, aspect. Historically they have much in common, but socially, psychologically, even geographically, they are very different. Belgium has nine million people packed into 11,775 square miles. Nowhere are its frontiers as much as two hundred miles apart. Belgium speaks two languages, French in Wallonia (the south), Flemish in Flanders. Brussels, the "little Paris" and capital, has nearly a million

(*Continued on page 161*)

LOCH NESS.

SCOTLAND

Overleaf: Pass of GLENCOE.

Near FORT WILLIAM: Black moors.

ENGLAND

STONEHENGE: Sunrise.

LONDON: Big Ben and Parliament Square.

Right: Tower Bridge and the Tower of London

Royal Guards at drill.

LONDON: St. Paul's Cathedral.

WINDSOR: St. George's Chapel in the Castle.

ETON: Boys on the way to class.

LONDON: Flea-market connoisseurs.

Right: YORK: In the old city.

STRATFORD-ON-AVON: Shakespeare Hotel (*above*) and Shakespeare's birthplace (*right*).

BLENHEIM: The Duke of Marlborough's park.

CAERNARVON: Edward I's castle.

NORVEGE

BERGEN : Le port et le marché aux poissons.

Ancient stave church.

Woman from Gudbrandsdal Valley.

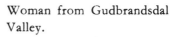

OSLO: Viking ship in the Folk Museum.

SWEDEN

STOCKHOLM: The old city.

WELLINGBY: A modern suburb of Stockholm.

Right: STOCKHOLM: Changing o
the Guard at the Royal Palace.

DROTTNINGHOLM: The castle.

STOCKHOLM: A guided
tour for children.

DROTTNINGHOLM: *Orpheus* performed in the castle theater.

STOCKHOLM: In Carl Milles' garden.

Right: VISBY: Towered walls of the old Hansa city.

ROTNEROS CASTLE: Site of the Goesta Berling saga.

VISBY: Chimney sweep on his morning rounds.

STOCKHOLM: When the fleet comes in.

LAPLAND: Lapps with reindeer calf.

FINLAND

HELSINKI: South harbor and government buildings.

A Finnish potter at the Arabia plant.

TAMPERE: Playing the kantele.

Right: Midsummer night's bonfire.

DENMARK

ELSINORE: Kronborg,
Hamlet's castle.

COPENHAGEN: Fishing boats and fishwives.

ODENSE: Egeskov castle
on the island of Fyn.

ODENSE: An old restaurant in town.

HILLEROD SOUND: Frederiksborg Castle.

Left: AERO. *Above:* Hans Andersen's house in ODENSE.

HOLLAND

GOUDA: Town Hall and church.

Right: HAARLEM: In the Frans Hals Museum

AMSTERDAM: Canal front.

SCHEVENINGEN: Mending nets.

DELFT: Reflections.

ROTTERDAM: Windmills on Kinderdyke.

Left: ALKMAAR:
Cheese market.

SCHEVENINGEN:
The sea front.

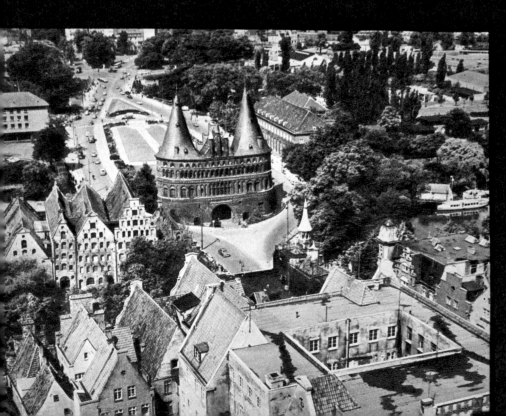

LUBECK: Old Hanseatic city.

COLOGNE: Watch on the Rhine.

Overleaf: NUREMBERG: Albrecht Dürer's house at right.

GERMANY

HEIDELBERG: University
students by the Neckar.

MUNICH: Hofbrähaus guest.

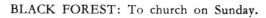

BLACK FOREST: To church on Sunday.

Bavarian couple.

Right: ROTHENBURG: Old gateways.

Overleaf: Country church near FUSSEN; MESPELBRUNN CASTLE.

GOLDENER HIRSCH

OBERAMMERGAU:
The Passion Play's St. Peter.

Right: BAVARIA: Kirche-in-der-Wies
(Church in the Meadow).

REGENSBURG: The first taxi.

BEAUNE: The old Hospice.

In the Burgundy country.

NORTHERN
FRANCE

DIJON: Local costume

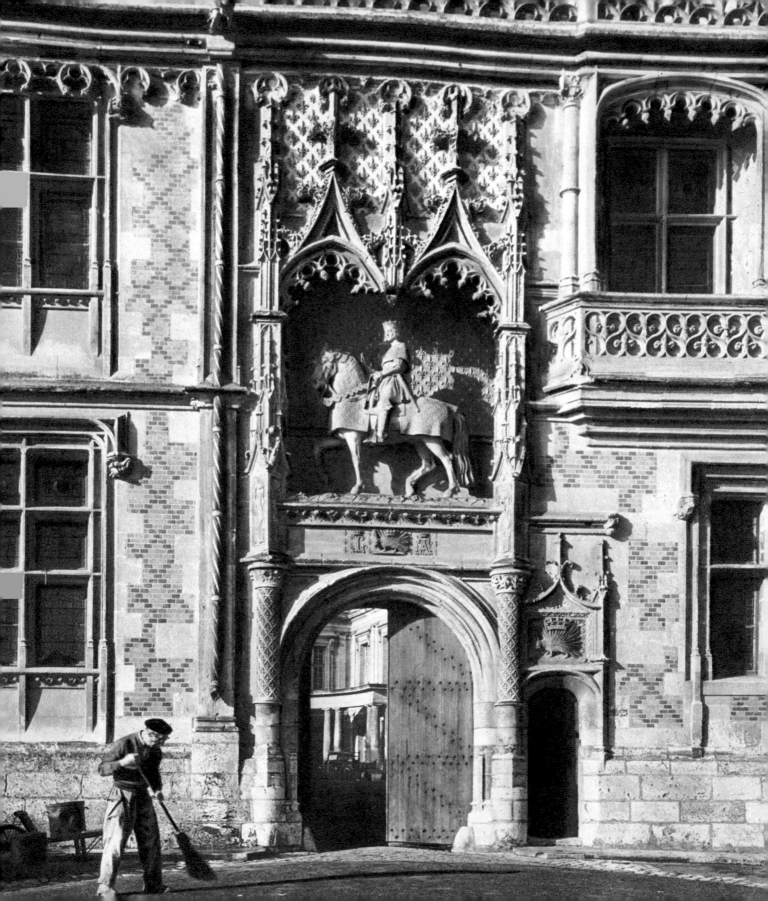

CHEVERNY: Drawing room in the Château on the Loire.

Left: BLOIS: Entrance to the Château with the figure of Louis XII.

CHAMBORD: Autumn leaves.

CHEVERNY: Meet of hounds.

Right: LE MOULIN: Swans on the moat.

PARIS: The River Seine and Notre Dame.

Tourists on the Left Bank.

Sunday morning in the Tuilerie

Paradise for painters.

Overleaf: PARIS: Place de la Concorde.

157

These two young Parisians are temporary, but their gesture (like the appeal of Paris) is eternal.

and a half population. Important from the eighth century on, Brussels was rebuilt after Marshal Villeroy's bombardment in 1695 and again after the fire of 1731. The Royal Palace and Palais de Justice were erected in the ninth century. The enchanting Grand' Place where the Hotel de Ville, the Broodhuis, begun in 1402, and the guild houses stand, is the city's chief showplace. Fine restaurants, cafés, and shops surround it. Inside the Hotel de Ville are magnificent ceiling paintings and tapestries designed by Victor Janssens. The Manneken Fountain, cast in bronze in 1619, is a city mascot, and the church of SS. Michael and Gudule with its heavenly stained glass of the thirteenth to fifteenth centuries, the Royal Palace, the "Bois," and the house of Erasmus in the suburb of Anderlecht are other sights that everyone goes to see.

Antwerp was a great port in the sixteenth century, and it still is. The city's architectural attractions include the splendid Gothic Cathedral, begun in 1352, which contains three great paintings by Rubens, and the Town Hall with its Renaissance façade. The Museum of Fine Arts contains other examples of Rubens' work and paintings by Memling, Brueghel, Van Dyck, and other Flemish and Dutch Masters.

Northwest of Brussels is the district of Ghent, famed for its orchids, azaleas and begonias, which are exported all over the world. At its center is the city of the same name, the capital of Flanders. Here are the Castle of the Counts, the Château of Gerard the Devil, the Hôtel de Ville, and the picturesque Beguinages or almshouses. In Ghent's cathedral stands the greatest triptych of all time, *The Adoration of the Lamb*, painted by the Van Eyck brothers between 1420 and 1432.

Farther northwest, en route to Ostend and the Belgian beaches, is Bruges, seventh-century "City of Bridges," once the pride of the Hanseatic League, and still one of the loveliest of towns anywhere. The medieval buildings and bridges (there are over fifty of them), the gateways, and swan-filled canals are enchanting. St. John's Hospital is where Memling lived and worked and where some of his best paintings hang. The thirteenth-century Beguinage, Notre Dame church, the Grand' Place at the foot of the belfry, St. Sauveur Cathedral, the Halles (market), Quai du Mirois and Lac d'Amour, all add to the historic charm of this capital of West Flanders.

From Brussels — or from anywhere in tiny Belgium — an easy trip through Namur will take you to the beautiful Ardennes Forest, extending from France through southern Belgium to the Rhineland. Here are magnificent views and good hunting. Also in the south is the Meuse River, with great country houses such as Dave, Freyr and Namêche. To the north, near the West German frontier, is Liège, Wallonia's intellectual and industrial center, with its coal and iron industries.

Everywhere in Belgium there are farms, producing one of the highest yields per acre in the world. And everywhere are battlefields — from Namur, with its Citadel fortified since the days the Belgae defied Caesar, to Waterloo, no longer the "dreary plain" Victor Hugo called it, and such battlefields of more recent history as Mons and Ypres. Twice in this century, and almost countless times before, Belgium has been invaded and despoiled. Yet it has recovered, now as always, economically and emotionally, and once more welcomes visitors warmly.

HOLLAND

Even in Roman days, Holland had its own culture, and the Batavians and Frisians were courageous and freedom-loving peoples, as today's Netherlanders still are, witness the long-drawn-out years of internal resistance to the Nazis from May 1940 to May 1945.

Amsterdam, Holland's biggest port, was already flourishing in 1300. Divided into ninety islands by a circular network of canals often more crowded with traffic than the streets, the city has some three hundred bridges which hold it together. Lovely seventeenth-century patrician houses rise along the canals or *grachten*, looking just as they do in old Dutch paintings. Reflections in the water — houses with stepped façades, churches with spires, arched bridges, flower stands bright with blossoms, shop windows, markets piles high with redcoated cheeses, and everywhere barges — make Amsterdam doubly colorful and inviting. The view down the canal at the point where the church of St. Nicholas stands is particularly picturesque.

Besides being one of the cleanest, most picturesque and "wateriest" cities in the world — Venice and Stockholm are its only competitors — Amsterdam is an industrial center, the world's diamond-cutting headquarters, and a great center of art besides. The Municipal Museum contains many Van Goghs; the Fodor Museum, French and Dutch pictures; and the justly renowned Rijksmuseum many of the best Rembrandts, including the *Night Watch*, as it is called, incredibly beautiful Vermeers, and canvases by Rubens, Brueghel, Hals, and other masters. Rembrandt came to Amsterdam from Leyden; Spinoza also lived here, and Erasmus, who said "his heart was Catholic and his stomach Lutheran," came here from his native Rotterdam to eat well (the city still has some of the best restaurants in the world) and poke fun at the citizens for living in trees like rooks because their houses were set on piles.

Gouda is a town as well as a cheese. But the real cheese center is Alkmaar, where more than ten thousand cheeses are weighed annually in the sixteenth-century Weigh House. Here Friday is market day, and dealer purchases are sealed by a *handslag*, for "a Netherlander's word sealed by a handclasp is his bond." The buildings and native costumes at Alkmaar are most picturesque; so too are those on the island of Marken and in the fishing village of Volendam, which is well worth visiting for its local Dutch flavor.

Besides cheeses and canals, Holland is famous for its windmills, for its tulip fields, which occupy a million of its acres, and for its blue and white pottery, which is still made at Delft — a city of pretty, clean houses sunning themselves on the canal banks. In Delft William the Silent was murdered in 1584, and Hugo Grotius, who invented the idea of neutrality, is buried. Near Delft is Rotterdam, much rebuilt since World War II and now a prosperous and bustling modern city.

Northeast of Delft is The Hague, the seat of the Dutch Government since Count Willem II in 1249 built the castle near the sea. Here the Queen lives and opens the Chambers of Parliament, in a colorful session at the old palace, once a year. Near to the city is Scheveningen, the famous beach resort, with its old quarters and a new fashionable side too, with quaint wicker chairs set like sentries on the beach. Art lovers go to the Mauritshuis to see the Rembrandts, the Van Goghs, and other good paintings. The biggest collection of Van Goghs, however, is across the country at the Kröller-Muller museum near Arnhem, scene of one of the fiercest battles of World War II. There are no less than two hundred and seventy works by Van Gogh here in a handsome modern gallery, designed by architect Henry van de Velde.

Leyden, Rembrandt's native town on the old Rhine, is the Oxford of Holland. The university, given to the city by William of Orange, was closed by the Nazis but now flourishes again with over a thousand students. Typical of Leyden are the old and attractive Hofjes (rent-free houses) grouped around courtyards. Surrounding the city and typical, too, are the bulb fields, windmills, and waterways. In icy winters there are canal races on skates; one, the Windmill Race, goes on — strength of the competitors permitting — for thirty-odd miles!

Utrecht also has a university, dating back to 1636, and, connected with it, a superb library in the Louis Bonaparte Palace, a museum of natural history, and a botanical garden. The Royal Mint is here, the superb Maliebaan — a triple avenue of lime trees — a museum of fine art, and one devoted to industrial art. Around the city are stretches of pretty country, lovely houses, and the old castle of Zuilen, cleverly restored in 1752.

Holland, with the highest longevity in Europe — seventy-one years — is highly industrialized, about forty per cent of the population being industrial workers. The shops are filled with tempting home-made objects, the clean restaurants with good food, the museums with first-rate pictures, the gardens with bulbs and flowers; all this and the wonderful canals and pretty, though flat landscape, make a tour of Holland one of the pleasantest experiences, and certainly one of the most sanitary.

WEST GERMANY

WEST GERMANY reaches from the North Sea to the Bavarian Alps, from Lübeck and the Schleswig-Holstein peninsula to Munich, and from Aachen to Eschwege. The country's economic recovery since World War II is staggering; industrial production in 1960 was 176 per cent more than that of 1936.

In the industrial north, Lübeck, Bremen, and Hamburg make up the trio of German Hanseatic ports. All have been restored since the last war and are booming. Cologne — the Roman city begun by Agrippa — was also a member of the Hanseatic League and is particularly famous for its cathedral, called the most impressive monument of German High Gothic style along the Rhine. A trip up the river could start here and should include the famous Rock whose echo started the legend of the Lorelei siren, set to rhyme by Heine, to music by Liszt. All up and down the Rhine valley are towns and cities with cathedrals and castles — Worms, the Nibelungen city, where the Diet attended by Luther was held; Speyer, where eight German Emperors lie buried in the Cathedral's crypt, and Xanten, which was Siegfried's city. All up and down the valley, too, are typical, charming German villages with half-timber houses, high pitched tiled roofs, inns with handsome heraldic signs, and vineyards along the river banks. This is the original land of "*Wein, Weib und Gesang*," which, with numerous variations, is sung over — or under — bottles of wine on both sides of the river, across the country and world.

Mainz, where many of the Rhine boat trips start or end, is the center of the German wine trade, and the city where Gutenberg invented printing. Frankfurt, modern except for the restored old quarter with the Roemer Hall, Goethe house and museum, is the scene of big exhibitions and international conventions like the Book Fair, held there late each autumn and attended by publishers and the book trade from everywhere under the sun. South is Heidelberg in the Neckar Valley, the picturesque city of *The Student*

Prince and home of the oldest university in Germany. Here in the castle courtyard, delightful serenades are held during the summer; here too are the thirteenth-century castle, the old Town Hall and the Palatine Museum.

Nuremberg, in the heart of Germany, is the home town of the *Meistersinger*, and the birthplace of Albrecht Dürer, greatest of German artists. In days of old, Nuremberg was the center of the toy-making trade and today it promises to become so once again. Here is held the oldest German Fair, the Christ Child's Mart. To the north is Bayreuth, where Wagner lived and where his grandsons stage an ultramodern music festival through July and August.

South Germany is a pride of ancient towns and villages. Rothenberg on the Tauber, with little red-roofed houses and narrow streets curled up inside the walls; Dinkelsbühl, with walls dating back to 928 and fairy-tale buildings; and Nördlingen, another picture-book town which came through two battles in the Thirty Years' War, form a romantic trio. Augsburg to the south is the city where the splendid Fuggers and Welsers lived luxuriously in the fifteenth and sixteenth centuries. The Welsers once owned all Venezuela; the Fuggers, merchant princes of enormous wealth, established the so-called Fuggerei in 1519, a town built within a city and the world's first social settlement.

Between Augsburg and Munich lies Oberammergau, noted for its elaborately painted houses and the Passion Play given every ten years by a cast of a thousand local performers to local music. Munich, gateway to the Bavarian Alps, is headquarters for the best beer in the world, Löwenbräu, and for Bavarian costumes and pipes. Near it, to the south, is the most famous of southern Germany's churches, Kirche-in-der-Wies, a white and gold wonder in the purest baroque. Even on a gray day the inside is a glory and on a sunny day here is yet more light. A mixture of romanesque and sheer fantasy is Neuschwanstein Castle, near the Austrian border, built by mad King Ludwig II. For the much lovelier rococo Linderhof Castle, Ludwig was also responsible; and in this region too lovely Nymphenburg Castle, built in 1663, and Herrenchiemsee, a copy of Versailles.

For a breathtaking journey, drive from Munich through the mountain-and-lake-filled country to Garmisch-Partenkirchen. The nearly ten-thousand-foot Zugspitze is nearby, and mountains throughout the area can be climbed or ascended by cogwheel railway and chair lift. On Lake Constance is lovely Meersburg; and still farther west is the Black Forest, renowned for its beauty and its cuckoo clocks. The dense dark woods abounding in silver fir form only a part of the hundred-mile-long stretch of the Black Forest range. In between are pastures and lakes, villages with thatched-roof cottages, and spas like Baden-Baden, to which the Romans went for its healing springs. These places are all connected by excellent roads.

Germany is a land of music, mountains, and festivals, of woods, lakes, and mountains, of medieval towns and modern cities and flourishing industries run by people of enormous energy and efficiency. The Germans are the best camera makers and printers in the world, and today everything they do seems to make them richer still.

NORTHERN FRANCE

AND so back to France, but to a very different part from southern France that dips its feet into the Mediterranean, dancing and sunning itself between Italy and Spain, the other two of the three Latin Graces.

Northern France is Celtic. Brittany, surrounded on three sides by the sea, is loved for its villages with their churches and Calvaries such as Plougastel-Daoulas and, better still, Guimiliau; for its megalithic monuments at Carnac and for the Breton *Pardons*, unique combinations of religious festival and fair, where people wear traditional regional costume, and a good time is had by all. In the Bay of Mont-Saint-Michel is the miracle shrine and fortress, connected with the mainland only at low tide.

In Normandy there are rural houses with thatched roofs, rich farmland and apple orchards that froth in April blossom, and fruit in September, and are used to produce cider and Calvados, a golden apple liqueur.

In Normandy, too, are the ports of Dieppe, Le Havre, and Cherbourg, and the beaches where many men died and where many men today with their womenfolk and children enjoy the surf and sea and sun and golden sands. Here are Honfleur, the fishing harbor at the mouth of the Seine, Trouville and fashionable Deauville.

Central France is castles and cathedrals and wine. The greatest vineyards in the world are in Burgundy, and the claret and champagne countries are hardly less precious. In Yonne is Chablis, where the famous white wine is produced, and Villenueve-sur-Yonne, which should be visited for its medieval fortifications. Vézelay, with its great Romanesque abbey, was founded in the ninth century. Here in 1146 St. Bernard preached the second crusade and from here, in 1190, Richard Coeur de Lion and Philip Augustus of France began the third. Nearby, in the Côte d'Or, is Beaune, with its lovely Gothic hospice supported by proceeds from its own superb vineyards. Dijon is a wonderful place to drink — and eat.

In the Loire country are set such gems of architecture as Chambord, the greatest château of all, which Francis I built in the sweet and lyrical landscape of Anjou, and Chenonceaux, on the Cher, which Henry II acquired and gave to his mistress Diane de Poitiers, who in turn had to relinquish it to Henry's wife Catherine de Médicis after the king died. It has an enchanting bridge. In 1747 Jean Jacques Rousseau was tutor at Chenonceaux and vastly enjoyed himself. Azay-le-Rideau and Chaumont (where Catherine de Médicis sent Diane de Poitiers after ousting her from Chenonceaux), and Chinon, Blois and rococo Chéverny are five other châteaux not to be missed. The town of Chinon, on the Vienne, is where Rabelais was born, where Richard Coeur de Lion died of wounds in 1199, and where in 1429 Joan of Arc fasted and prayed before setting forth as "one sent by God" to campaign against the English. Angers, chief town of Maine-et-Loire, lies with its castle a few miles above the confluence of the two rivers. Near it are Solesmes, the Benedictine Abbey where Gregorian music is best sung, and Saumur, between Angers and Tours, home of the greatest riding school in France. Tours, the town of St. Martin, was invaded by the Germans in 1870 and 1940. Nantes too was badly hurt in World War II but is now itself again and a delightful seaport. Nearby is the "Emerald Coast" (and off it, such romantic islands as Noirmoutier, d'Yeu and de Ré) on the way down through La Rochelle to Bordeaux, from which a ride into Dordogne will take you to one of the great ancient wonders of France — the Lascaux caves, with their fantastic prehistoric murals discovered by two boys falling into a hole there as recently as 1940.

The greatest Gothic cathedral in the world is at Chartres, where the stained glass, removed in wartime, has become our thermometer of peace. This supreme example of Gothic architecture attracts millions of visitors, and thousands walk there annually in pilgrimage from Paris. Outside Paris too — in separate directions — are Versailles, with the gigantic palace and gardens of the Sun King Louis XIV, whose brilliant ceremonies made it the glittering model for all the other courts of Europe, and Fontainebleau, with its lovely palace.

And so to Paris, which, more than any other capital, is the epitome of the whole country. Paris has been the capital of France since about 505, and is supremely good at it. It is most feminine of cities as Rome is the most masculine, the gayest as Rome is the grandest. Paris and Rome are bracketed like a well-matched, long-married pair.

In Paris, a good day could begin by going to Les Halles, the great market, and afterward to a sung Mass at Notre Dame. The great cathedral brooding over the Seine, with its gargoyles, is near the Pantheon, where Voltaire and Rousseau are buried, and St. Etienne du Mont, where Ste. Geneviève's gold shrine is. The Cluny Museum is excellent for a wet day; the Louvre lights up the winged victory of Samothrace by night, and crowds stand rooted in front of the Mona Lisa by day. The traffic-filled Place de la Concorde is almost more dangerous today for pedestrians than it once was for the Kings and peers like Louis XVI, Marie Antoinette, Robespierre, and the twenty-eight hundred others who lost their heads there in the Revolution. The *Arc de Triomphe* is the heart of Paris, and the flame here to the memory of the Unknown Soldier of World War I is re-lit nightly.

The Sainte Chapelle, built by St. Louis to house the Crown of Thorns, is a shell of stained glass, beached when the waters of faith receded; St. Germain des Prés, the oldest church in Paris, is close to the university and famous cafés like the *Deux Magots*, where painters and writers (especially existentialists) congregate.

The quays are still glorious for browsing among the books and prints displayed for sale there, and the statue-and-fountain-filled Paris gardens — the Tuileries, the Luxembourg, Vincennes, the Bois — are an integral part of the city, not refuges from it. Magic names, too, and magical places and landmarks are the Champs Elysées, the Rond Point, the Eiffel Tower, the Pont Neuf and Pont Royal, the Invalides, Montmartre, the Sacré Coeur, the Rue de la Paix and the Place Vendôme, center of the *couturiers*, all separate — and together conjuring up visions of this most painted, proud and perfect city.

A NOTE FOR PHOTOGRAPHERS

THERE is no better way to re-experience the pleasures of a holiday than by looking at your own travel photographs. Color postcards are easy to come by so, if you intend to take a camera with you, why not try for something different and distinctive in your own work? Instead of taking a full view of the Eiffel Tower or Piazza San Marco, for instance, you might shoot it through a doorway or window, or find some other interesting foreground detail. And by all means vary your collection with other types of shots — of cafés, shops, faces, and other intimate, characteristic details that contribute to the general atmosphere of each place you visit.

Even if your time schedule is short, try to make the acquaintance of one or two local people — an innkeeper, perhaps, a street vendor, a museum guard, or a curious child. Your pictures of them, related to their own place and time, will probably turn out to be the most interesting ones. And if your family is with you, make them work as natural, unposed models in appropriate settings.

A story of your trip, with a beginning, an end, and clear continuity in between, will add fascination to a showing of the pictures later. The element that holds such a story together is a feeling of movement from one place to another in orderly fashion — for example, a shot of the border crossing between sequences on two different nationalities, or pictures from a plane window with recognizable landmarks at the beginning and end of a flight.

You cannot expect only sunny days, but clouds and rain shouldn't ruin your sightseeing or picture-taking. The camera can be protected from showers under the flap of a raincoat, and a light-yellow or skylight filter can be used over the lens. The quality of the light just before or after a storm is matchless. Even during a downpour you can get wonderfully evocative pictures by shooting from a sheltered spot — under an awning, or in a doorway. And after the rain, both city and countryside take on a fresh and glistening quality. Also plan on taking some pictures early in the morning and in late afternoon or at night. The quality of early and late light can be more dramatic than the bright midday sun, and such pictures will provide contrast in your collection. For night or indoor work you will need a tripod. If you find carrying one — even the smallest collapsible variety — too much of an encumbrance, the next best thing is a clamp with tripod socket, which can be fixed to a fence, wall, or door to hold the camera.

Everyone should give as much thought to composition and lighting as time allows before taking each picture, and should keep his equipment simple enough to be master of it at all times; otherwise the best moment for a picture may have passed before he is ready.

There are many good cameras, both small and large, from which to choose, and everyone has a favorite. The Rolleiflex has been my camera for thirty years. I carry four of them — two standard models, the Tele-Rollei, and the Wide Angle. On my last European trip I also used the Brooks-Plaubel Veriwide 100, with which most of the two-page horizontal pictures in this book were made. It has the Schneider Super-Angulon lens that sees an angle of 100 degrees. Much of the high cost of a camera is in the quality of lens. Rolleiflexes, for instance, are fitted with 80-mm Schneider Xenotar lenses which give a clear-sharp image and correct color. This is not to say that excellent pictures cannot be made with inexpensive cameras, but for people who want quality there is no substitute for a good lens and precise mechanism. Few non-professionals will want as many cameras as I do, but it is worth carrying two if possible — one loaded with black-and-white film and one with color, so you can choose the most suitable film for each subject.

My own choices of film were Kodak Ektachrome and Tri-X Pan. The latter is fast, but I use it at a lower speed rating than the manufacturer recommends, and find it gives excellent quality and fine grain. Kodachrome is also good, and Kodacolor gives you prints instead of slides. Exposure charts come with the film, and I suggest you take more than one picture of each important subject, varying the exposure up or down one stop to give yourself margin for error.

There can be no rules that determine whether to shoot a particular picture in color or in black and white. It is important to respect both media, for there is no such thing as "*only* a black and white." And at night, you can seldom work with color. In this book there is no page in black and white which I would have preferred in color, and none in color that I feel was as good in black and white.

FRITZ HENLE

168

1